Informal Credit Markets
and the New Institutional Economics:
The Case of Philippine Agriculture

Informal Credit Markets
and the New Institutional Economics:
The Case of Philippine Agriculture

Sagrario L. Floro
and
Pan A. Yotopoulos

Westview Press
BOULDER, SAN FRANCISCO & OXFORD

Copyright © 1991 by Westview Press, Inc.

Published in 1991 in the United States of America by Westview Press, Inc., 5500 Central Avenue, Boulder, Colorado 80301, and in the United Kingdom by Westview Press, 36 Lonsdale Road, Summertown, Oxford OX2 7EW

Library of Congress Cataloging-in-Publication Data
Floro, Sagrario L.
   Informal credit markets and the new institutional economics : the case of Philippine agriculture / Sagrario L. Floro and Pan A. Yotopoulos.
   p. cm.
   Includes index.
   ISBN 0-8133-8136-3
   1. Agricultural credit—Philippines. 2. Philippines—Industries, Rural—Finance. 3. Credit—Philippines. 4. Informal sector (Economics)—Philippines. I. Yotopoulos, Pan A.   II. Title.
HD1440.P5Y68 1991
332.7'1'09599—dc20   90-49978
                                                              CIP

Printed and bound in the United States of America

   The paper used in this publication meets the requirements of the American National Standard for Permanence of Paper for Printed Library Materials Z39.48-1984.

10   9   8   7   6   5   4   3   2   1

For our daughters

Maria-Jennifer
and Kyvele-Rhea,
respectively,

S.L.F.
P.A.Y.

Contents

Tables and Figures

Figures

Foreword

The 1970s and the 1980s saw a quiet revolution in economic theory and a concomitant change in economic policy. The idea that less developed countries (LDC's) could quickly be transformed into more developed countries by a process of rapid capital accumulation and industrialization, all guided by central planning, has been abandoned. It has gradually dawned upon governments and their economic advisors that if the plight of the majority of the population, those living within the rural sector, is to be improved within their lifetime, agricultural productivity must be increased. While the new seeds of the Green Revolution have put the prospects of that within the reach of many, it has become apparent that if farmers within the LDC's are to take full advantage of the potentials of modern technologies, they must have access to credit. Providing credit within the rural sector has thus become a matter of priority.

There is concern not only about the availability of credit, but also the terms at which it is provided. High interest rates not only discourage productivity investments, but also serve to redistribute income from the poorer peasants to the better-off moneylenders.

While a number of governments have, accordingly, made an attempt to extend formal credit institutions into the rural sector, they have had only limited success: they have not driven out the informal moneylenders. More surprisingly, competition between the two has not even led to significantly lower interest rates. This has represented a puzzle for traditional economics.

The advances in theoretical economics of the past fifteen years have provided a framework for addressing this and other puzzling aspects of rural credit markets. This work has stressed the importance of costly and imperfect information, and has argued that many of the important institutions in any economy can be interpreted as responses to these information problems.

One of the most fruitful applications of what is variously called Information Economics or the New Institutional Economics has been to credit markets. Exchanges in credit markets are distinctly different from exchanges in other markets: money today is given up in exchange for a *promise* in the future. Such promises are frequently broken: the borrower defaults on his loan. Central problems of the institutions within the credit market are thus to enforce loan contracts, to sort out those more likely to pay from those less likely to pay, and to provide incentives and control mechanisms which make it more likely that borrowers undertake safer actions, thus increasing the likelihood of repayment.

Problems of information imperfections are particularly pervasive and important within LDC's. Rural credit markets thus provide a particularly fertile forum within which to test out some of the basic ideas of the Information Economics/New Institutional Economics. But more is at stake than just testing a new theory: the new theories have the hope of providing a framework for understanding rural credit markets. Such an understanding is necessary if we are to devise sensible policies with respect to the rural credit market.

This book provides the first comprehensive study of rural credit markets within the new paradigm. It provides a rare combination of a significant development of the theory and a test of the theory on newly gathered data. The theory not only holds up remarkably well in this laboratory-of-real-life test, but provides deep insights into the workings of what is shown to be a most complex market. The book will provide food for thought for development economists – both theorists and policymakers – for years to come.

I do not want to repeat the major results and findings of the study: the introductory and concluding chapters do an admirable job. In the remaining paragraphs of this foreword, I want to call attention to a few of the most striking, puzzling, or disturbing findings.

The study corroborates other studies which have found that informal moneylenders are at the center of rural credit markets – accounting for 90% or more of all money lent. It also corroborates the high interest rates charged. What is more surprising, however, is that it shows that interest rates do not necessarily rise with default rates. The theories that the authors present provide insights into why this might be so.

The authors point out that both the heterogeneity of lenders and the heterogeneity of borrowers are important for understanding the functioning of rural credit markets. Different lenders have different information about different borrowers, and have different objectives in making loans. Commercial lenders are thus also concerned about the sales of their goods. More disturbingly, large farmers may be interested in encouraging indebtedness as a means of acquiring control of more land: for them, default may be a favorable outcome. The heterogeneity of lenders – and the limited information available to each – means that interest rates will not be equalized even across borrowers of similar characteristics by credit rationing. The authors provide ample evidence on each of these predictions of the theory.

Formal lending institutions face the same problems of sorting, incentives, and enforcement that informal lenders do, and in many ways they are at a disadvantage. They do not have access to the type of information that is a by-product of the interlinked relationships characterizing informal credit markets, where the lender may, for instance, have other commercial relationships with the borrower. One important suggestion of the study is that rather than viewing formal lending institutions and informal institutions as substitutes, as has been done in the past, they should be viewed as complements. Providing additional funds to large moneylenders to lend to smaller moneylenders, to lend to still smaller moneylenders, to lend ... eventually to farmers (the authors refer to this as credit layering) may be a more effective way of providing funds to the rural sector. Whether competition among lenders is sufficiently keen that such a trickling down process will result in lower interest rates is problematical; but even if interest rates do not fall more credit may be made available and the additional credit may be more efficiently allocated than if the formal institutions were to try to do the sorting, monitoring, and enforcement on their own. In short, the informal credit institutions may have a comparative advantage in these activities, and if that is the case, the formal credit institutions should make use of it.

The authors end on an important note:

> Lending to small farmers in particular becomes extremely risky and costly under conditions that are only too familiar in underdevelopment and poverty: absence of transport links and of support infrastructures like irrigation in many rural areas, unfavorable terms of trade for the agricultural sector, and uneven access to land and modern agricultural inputs. Remedying these deficiencies improves the overall economic viability of small borrowers which in the final analysis determines the reach of the formal and the effectiveness of both formal and informal financial intermediation.

The development of rural credit markets and the development of the economy are inextricably interlinked.

Joseph E. Stiglitz
Stanford

Preface

The conventional wisdom about credit markets has been radically altered in recent years through the introduction of elements of moral hazard, adverse selection of risk, and quality-price relationships. Important empirical studies have been published which are leading to vastly different policy implications. This analysis has not been explicitly extended to informal credit markets so far, although it is widely recognized that credit transacted outside the banking circuit is quantitatively huge and qualitatively critical, especially in developing countries.

This book combines the new theoretical approach to credit markets with certain precepts of the New Institutional Economics in order to analyze informal credit markets. While the formal financial institutions in developing countries carry out credit transactions within the limits set by the market environment and by government policies, informal institutions evolve by a particular selection of modes of economic behavior which are responses to intrinsic imperfections of the market. The informal sector enhances trust by making existing ties an integral component of credit contracts: the contractual component of informal credit capitalizes on the personalistic (social and economic) relationships between the transacting parties.

The implications of the New Institutional Economics approach for the informal credit markets are formulated as testable hypotheses and tested with a sample of informal credit contracts in the Philippines. More specifically, the implications of quantity rationing and excess demand for credit are empirically investigated in order to answer a number of questions: What are the interest rates prevailing in the informal market and how are they determined? What are the important non-price covenants in the credit contract? How is the problem of asymmetric information between the contracting parties solved? How are borrowers rendered observationally equivalent in the absence of collateral? How does interlinkage of credit with another market operate to offset the adverse-selection-of-risk effect?

The conclusions of this work extend beyond the role that the informal credit sector plays in the process of development. They refer also to important public policy issues that relate to the operation of the formal credit sector, such as liberalization of interest rates and deregulation.

The potential audience of this work includes the analysts, students, and practitioners of economic development, along with the policy makers and the public who are concerned with credit markets and issues of interest rate liberalization and bank deregulation.

The list of our creditors in this work is substantial. We would formally like to acknowledge our informal indebtedness to them. The International Rice Research Institute provided financial and technical support for conducting the sample survey in 1983-84. The indefatigable support and insights provided by farmers, innumerable Filipino organizations, and financial intermediaries sharpened our critical understanding of the operations of informal credit markets. The Development Center, Organization for Economic Cooperation and Development, supported our early research and published a first report on the subject. The Development Research Institute, Tilburg University, The Netherlands, extended a few months' research professorship to Yotopoulos and helped him test a number of the ideas by providing funds for organizing a colloquium on "The Role of the New Institutional Economics in Economic Development: Primrose Path or Dead-End Alley?" The Institute of Economic Research, Kyoto University, also provided a research professorship for 1988-89, which was in part invested in this project. Our students at the American University and Stanford, respectively, were exposed to a course and a seminar on the topic, and provided both intellectual mortar and constructive criticism. We also profited from comments by Dale Adams, Tim Besley, Amit Bhaduri, Christina David, Emmanuel Esguerra, Dimitris Germidis, Donald Harris, Christine Jones, Ruud Picavet, Debraj Ray, Michael Roemer and Terry Sicular. An all-Filipino team was responsible for the index, bibliography and desk-top publishing: Dina Umali, Manuel Gaspay, and Ricky Pascual. Finally, Steve Wahlstrom and Mary Yotopoulos deserve much more than this perfunctory-sounding spousal acknowledgment.

Sagrario L. Floro
Pan A. Yotopoulos
Stanford

1

Introduction

The role of monetary and financial institutions is fundamental for economic development. The introduction of money and credit reduces the costs of exchange and transactions and extends the market for goods and services and the scope of the division of labor. Completing *co-temporal* transactions in goods and services through the intermediation of money, as opposed to barter, is yet another demonstration of a non-Euclidean world where the most direct line between two points is not necessarily the shortest (least expensive) distance (option). Expanding the principle of indirect exchange of goods and services to *inter-temporal* markets leads to credit and finance. The existence of a capital market decreases the transaction costs in time as the existence of money (or transportation, for that matter) decreases the transaction costs in space. There has been an understandable emphasis in economic development, as a result, on extending the reach of credit markets through the expansion of (formal) financial intermediation (Goldsmith 1969).

This simple analogy between the role of money in co-temporal transactions and the role of credit in inter-temporal transactions has led one strand of the literature to apply to credit market analysis the orthodox economics framework of supply and demand. The existence of excess demand for credit, therefore, has been traditionally interpreted as evidence of temporary disequilibrium due to "financial repression" or other forms of government-imposed ceilings on the price of credit. Another trend in the literature emphasizes the non-homogeneity of borrowers on the basis of risk. The focus in this case is on extending the reach of financial markets by rendering the potential borrowers equivalent through the provision of collateral or security.

Credit in Economic Development

The argument has become recently more complicated with the emergence of various strands in the economics literature that have direct or indirect applicability on credit markets.

Credit in developing countries (LDC's) is transacted in markets that are inherently imperfect. Borrowers of varying kinds obtain funds from different types of lenders. Moreover, credit relationships are often complex, involving collateral arrangements and other kinds of restrictive covenants, such as market interlinkage. The key issue is whether such "structural distortions" are due to inefficient government regulation and insufficient collective action, or instead are the result of institutional responses aimed at overcoming incentive problems in credit market relationships. To a certain extent they reflect both factors.

Credit involves a relationship between the lender and the borrower, that contains the promise to repay in the future. The transaction is completed only when the loan plus interest is fully paid up at a future date. Since there is no humanly infallible way to gauge the true intentions of the borrower, the credit transaction entails trust in a significant way. Trust is the antidote to the existence of asymmetric information between lender and borrower that breeds moral hazard and adverse selection of risk. Fragmented credit markets then may be the result of institutional responses to overcoming incentive problems by building up trust. This is the domain of the New Institutional Economics.[1]

On the other hand, issues of trust in credit transactions are handled, especially in developed countries (DC's), through the classical attempts of perfecting the market by making potential borrowers homogeneous. For instance, collateral requirement, which makes a class of borrowers observationally indistinguishable, enhances trust. Improved social infrastructure, which makes the collateral clause enforceable at low transaction cost, builds confidence in the market exchange; so do various other trust-building mechanisms. Information-sharing networks between lenders, such as credit reference checks, reduce the otherwise prohibitive costs of gathering information. These responses lie in the province of increasing government efficiency and improving collective action.

Whatever the merits of the government efficiency approach, it can at best cover only a small part of the credit transactions in LDC's, those of the formal financial sector. The residual component of credit transacted in informal markets is systematically, and directly, related to the level of underdevelopment. Underdeveloped social infrastructure and poverty that make collateral unavailable are real issues in the developing world. The absence of market infrastructural support makes it difficult for lenders to obtain information and to rely on effective enforcement mechanisms. Trust cannot be readily established, severely constraining the area of operations of the formal financial intermediation sector. Thus formal credit leaves a vacuum that the informal sector comes to fill.

The issue of market imperfections and of institutional responses to overcoming incentive problems is distinct from the issue of equilibrium in the credit market. Moral hazard and adverse selection of borrowers, however, can lead to disequilibrium in the sense that price may not clear the credit market as Freimer and Gordon (1965), Jaffe and Russell (1976) and Stiglitz and Weiss (1981) have suggested. The latter separate the notion of equilibrium from the mechanism of price closure, the automatic process of equating supply and demand if prices do their job.[2] They have shown, instead, that when the expected quality of a commodity is a function of its price, equilibrium may be characterized by rationing, i.e., quantity closure (the "price-quality theorem"). In credit markets characterized by excess demand, an increase in the rate of interest for the purpose of equating supply and demand is likely to affect the quality of the loan by decreasing its probability of repayment. This may happen in two ways: First, past some critical rate of interest, high-quality borrowers either will seek credit elsewhere or will leave the market altogether. This leaves the lenders who charge high interest rates with a preponderance of borrowers who have high probability of default (adverse selection of risk effect). Second, the higher the interest rate, the greater is the attraction for the borrower of the more risky projects, and thus the greater the probability of default (incentive effect). Both effects imply a non-monotonic relationship between the expected return of the loan and the interest rate, with the former increasing less rapidly than the latter, and beyond a certain point declining. This means that the lender will engage in credit rationing — sorting among seemingly indistinguishable borrowers. Quantity rationing, in turn, implies that: (1) among seemingly identical applicants, some receive loans, and some do not; and/or (2) given the supply of credit, there exist identifiable groups of individuals who are unable to obtain loans, irrespective of the interest rate they are willing to pay.

This leads to the conclusion reached by Stiglitz and Weiss that there exists an optimum rate of interest that the lender charges, which is below the market-clearing rate of interest. In a situation where quantity rationing becomes an intrinsic feature of the credit market, how is the sorting of potential borrowers achieved? The fact that credit allocation does not operate through price-clearing strongly suggests that the interest rate is not the only important covenant in the credit contract. Is collateral another term in the credit contract that achieves the full sorting of borrowers?[3]

Stiglitz and Weiss extend their price-quality theorem to cover also collateral, in the sense that increasing the collateral requirement beyond an optimum point again leads to adverse selection of risk. This happens under three specific circumstances. The first case is when borrowers have the same amount of equity, and there are increasing returns to scale in production so that the smaller projects have a higher probability of failure. Since collateral increases the debt-equity ratio of a given project, the probability that the smaller, and default-prone, projects are undertaken increases. The second situation is when potential borrowers have different equity and all projects require the same investment. Controlling for the amount of collateral required, the presumption is that wealthy borrowers may be those who in the past have succeeded in risky endeavors and thus are less risk-averse. Conversely, the more conservative investors who have invested in safe projects are less able to furnish a given amount of collateral. Finally, the adverse selection of risk effect of the collateral may offset its direct positive effect in another general case, even if there are no increasing returns to scale in production and all individuals have the same utility function. Assuming that the wealthier individuals are also less risk-averse, one would expect that those who can put up the most capital in collateral are also willing to take the greatest amount of risk. Under some plausible conditions, the risk effect can be so strong as to lower the lender's expected return. The above cases illustrate clearly that interest rate cum collateral are still not sufficient for the full sorting of borrowers.

In the specific application to LDC's collateral as a covenant to the credit contract has been subjected to a specific institutional change to overcome other incentive problems that arise. It emerges in the form of market interlinkage, which is yet another subfield of the new institutional economics.[4]

The Role of the Informal Sector and the Plan of This Book

As the preceding bird's-eye-view of some salient ideas of the new institutional economics has suggested, various strands of this literature have been already applied to the analysis of credit markets. However, the discourse so far has remained at an abstract level. There has been no empirical study of the credit market that is cast entirely within the modern theoretical framework.[5]

The purpose of this book is to carry out the empirical investigation of credit markets beyond the point of price adjustments and collateral requirements (in the spirit of the Stiglitz-Weiss price-quality theorem) and within the context of the new institutional economics. This becomes especially important for understanding the role of informal financial intermediation where the contractual dimensions of credit build on the existing personalistic (social and economic) relationships between individuals. While the formal financial institutions in developing countries carry out credit transactions within the limits set by the market environment and by government policies, informal institutions evolve by a particular selection of modes of economic behavior that are responses to the intrinsic imperfections of the market. The informal sector enhances trust, i.e., confidence in the borrower's delivery of payment in the future, by making existing ties an integral component of credit contracts.

The preceding discussion highlighted quantity rationing and excess demand for credit as inherent characteristics of the market. The unanswered question is what completes the sorting of non-homogeneous borrowers in the competition among non-homogeneous lenders? This raises other interesting corollary questions: What are the other important non-price covenants in the credit contract? How is the problem of asymmetrical information between the contracting parties solved? How are borrowers rendered observationally equivalent in the absence of collateral? How does interlinkage of credit with another market operate to offset the adverse selection of risk effect? What is the optimum rate of interest that a maximizing lender is likely to charge?

Within a principal-agent framework, the price-quality theorem of Stiglitz-Weiss predicts that both the principal (lender) and the agent (borrower) can influence by their actions the probability of default. How is this evidenced in the case of different types of principal-agent relationships? Chapter 2 formulates the loose strands of the price-quality hypothesis of credit markets in developing countries in terms of testable propositions, specifically for the informal-sector credit.

The data used for verifying the testable hypotheses regarding informal credit were collected in a sample survey of over 100 borrower agricultural households and a number of informal-sector lenders drawn from 14 villages in three provinces of the Philippines in 1984.[6] The tests are formulated and the results reported in Chapters 3 to 6.

The role that the informal sector plays in filling in the credit vacuum left by the formal-sector rationing is formulated in terms of the residuality hypothesis in Chapter 3. This is illustrated with the historical experience of the Philippines. Furthermore, the issue of informal credit in general is formulated within the new institutional economics approach. The personalistic relationship developed between lenders and borrowers, it is argued, proposes to handle the problem of adverse selection of risk. It renders potential lenders observationally equivalent, and it completes the sorting process, given the maximization function of the lender. The implications of the new institutional economics approach to the credit market are formulated as testable hypotheses and pursued further in the subsequent chapters.

Chapter 4 distinguishes two types of lenders, trader-lenders and farmer-lenders, who face non-homogeneous borrowers. It builds the respective theoretical maximization models with market interlinkage for each type of lender. The specific sorting of borrowers as well as interest rate implications for each model are also formulated. Chapter 5 carries out the empirical analysis of interlinked credit for each type of lender and estimates the respective interest charges using the data from our survey sample. Chapter

6 empirically analyzes the sorting behavior and formulates explicitly the rationing rules that apply to each lender-type.

Finally, Chapter 7 draws the conclusions and the policy implications of the study.

Notes

1. For a concise statement of the domain of the New Institutional Economics see Langlois (1986), Eliasson (1986), Nabli and Nugent (1989a), Nabli and Nugent (1989b), Datta and Nugent (1989).

2. The remainder of this section draws heavily on Stiglitz and Weiss (1981).

3. Binswanger (1978, 1982) and Umbeck and Chatfield (1982) introduced collateral as a component in the credit contract. They perceive this form of contingency clause as a risk-sharing device that plays a major role in the lenders' sorting process.

4. For a good sample of this literature see Bardhan (1989a,b), and especially Bell and Srinivasan (1989) and Ray and Sengupta (1989).

5. For example, Datta and Nugent (1989) who conduct an exhaustive review of the literature of the new institutional economics do not cite a single empirical application in the credit market.

6. See Appendix for a description of the sampling procedure and the survey conducted to obtain the data.

2

Informal Financial Intermediation:
A New Institutional Economics
Perspective

The study of the nature of credit markets and the understanding of the way they work have attracted growing interest in recent years. Studies of formal financial intermediation (FFI) have revealed an asymmetry in the mobilization of potential savings and in the extension of credit.[1] In many cases, FFI is shown to be better suited to service the needs of big clients (in terms of asset value and loan demand) rather than small; it is more visible in the urban environment than in the rural; and it is more active in manufacturing than in agriculture. This asymmetry is viewed as evidence that the FFI sector operates in fragmented markets where competition is imperfect. The fragmentation of markets is commonly attributed to distortions imposed from the outside, the government.

While this view has some merit, the emphasis in this chapter is on the existence of transaction costs, that are inherent in the nature of financial intermediation and which lead to structural distortions in the credit market. The externalities created by these market distortions put a heavy restraint on the activities of the FFI sector; at the same time, they provide an opportunity for informal financial intermediation (IFI) to fill in the institutional vacuum left by the FFI sector. This chapter presents an overview of the prevailing schools of thought concerning the nature of credit markets in developing countries, namely, the traditional school and the financial repression school, and contrasts them with the new institutional economics approach. The residuality approach to IFI is formulated in an operational fashion in this chapter as well so that it can be specifically modeled in Chapter 4 and tested in Chapter 5.

The Traditional Approach to Capital Markets in LDC's

The imperfection that limits the role of financial intermediation in the capital market of developing countries, according to this school of thought, lies on the supply side of capital funds, savings. The traditional approach implicitly assumes that low levels of income limit the savings potential in LDC's. The role of government in increasing savings, creating credit, and providing incentives for the proper sectoral allocation of the limited loanable funds, as a result, becomes crucial.[2]

On the demand side, credit is considered an important input of production, and unavailability of credit lies at the heart of stagnant or low growth, inadequate capital formation, and limited investment opportunities. There is an implicit assumption that growth hinges on capital accumulation and that additional capital, via the credit market, would either promote or facilitate a more rapid rate of economic development (Cairncross 1962, Bottomley 1964). The economic performance of agriculture, in particular, has lagged behind in developing countries in terms of productivity, output, and income levels because of insufficient credit supply. The market rate of interest, moreover, is too high for small borrowers (Wai 1956, 1957, Bottomley 1964). This further constrains them in making capital investments that are necessary for increasing productivity. The high rates of interest in the credit market are also considered to be exploitative for they allow private lenders to earn monopoly rents.

Having dismissed the role of price incentives on the supply side of savings, the traditional approach relies heavily on input price incentives. Credit is treated as one of the production inputs; a reduction in the level of the interest rate lowers the cost of this input and provides the much needed incentive to productive capital formation. This in turn accelerates the adoption of improved technology and stimulates production. In this regard, the traditional school advocates cheap credit policies implemented through interest rate ceilings, anti-usury laws, and interest rate subsidies. The resulting imbalance between quantity demanded and quantity supplied at the non-equilibrium interest rate is addressed through quantity closure, credit rationing. The role of government credit programs becomes important in targeting interventions to specific sectors, especially agriculture, and to specific producers, especially the small enterprises, which are most vulnerable to the capital market imperfections.

The Financial Repression Approach

The financial repression school disputes the claims of the traditional school. While both schools perceive credit markets as fragmented and imperfect, the financial repression school argues that this is more a result of government policies which have repressed the growth of credit markets rather than an inherent characteristic of the market itself. The endemic distortions that characterize financial markets in developing countries are largely due to the manipulation of free-market prices by governments (McKinnon 1973, Shaw 1973). The low (often negative) interest rates that prevail in formal lending disrupt the supply side of the financial system and distort the loan demand, thereby directing the flow of credit to larger borrowers and to those with political clout and patronage.

The thesis of financial repression deals both with the supply of savings and the demand for credit sides of financial markets. On the supply side, the thesis rests on the proposition that individual savers respond to the reward of holding financial assets, conditional on the risk of holding these assets. The reward is the interest rate on savings and the risk of holding financial assets is the rate of inflation. The "interest rate elasticity" approach prescribes, therefore, high real interest rates and price stability as the means for eliciting savings. Cheap credit, in contrast, stifles the growth of formal financial institutions. Because of interest rate ceilings, banks cannot increase their resources through savings mobilization; they depend largely for loanable funds on the Central Bank rediscounting window. As such, they become mere conduits of government funds, and not mobilizers of rural savings.

The supply of savings is linked to the demand for investment through the postulated existence of ample investment opportunities in traditional agriculture with high rates of return — far exceeding the high levels of real interest rates (McKinnon 1973). The problem of modern technology, it is asserted, is indivisibility. While the farmer with only a small amount of investible funds can purchase traditional technology with low returns, he instantly gets access to modern technology (for example, a tractor) and hence, high rates of return once his accumulated savings exceed a minimum threshold level. The high interest rates, therefore, encourage deposits and do not necessarily stifle investment.

In any event, the low, non-equilibrium levels of interest rate have serious implications regarding the misallocation of resources. Gonzales-Vega (1980, 1984a), Adams (1984) and others have argued that a low-interest rate policy creates an excess demand for loans, building up arbitrage pressure and necessitating non-price allocation mechanisms. This makes "cheap credit" provided by banks to be not so cheap when other costs are also considered. Although the nominal interest rate may be low, out-of-pocket costs and opportunity costs of the borrower's time spent on carrying out loan procedures could be very high. Cheap credit also leads to a situation in which large borrowers get large loans and small borrowers get slowly rationed out, so the subsidized resources are cornered by the better-off group. Gonzales-Vega (1984b) concludes that with a constrained interest rate, financial institutions redistribute their credit portfolios in favor of larger, more established borrowers over smaller, riskier clients. Cheap credit has also opened new doors for monopoly rent seekers. Government suppression of bank interest rates below the market rates leads not only to inefficiency and distortions in the market, but also to discrimination against the poor and gives rise to opportunities for corruption and favoritism (Von Pischke and Adams 1983: 10).

The policy conclusions that follow from the financial repression thesis are financial liberalization, deregulation, and the removal of government intervention from all aspects of financial markets. These include refraining from all forms of price manipulations, such as interest rate ceilings, credit quotas, loan targeting, and interest subsidies. Loan supervision also comes under attack as having a repressive effect on the adoption of new technology and on the level of investment. More specifically, the financial repression school questions the attempts of the government to include loans as part of a package of inputs, arguing that packaging loans and using similar non-market rationing devices destroys the most attractive property of credit: fungibility. A special credit program, for example, may not achieve its desired results, say increase production investment, since target borrowers can divert cheap credit to consumption or to non-priority, yet more profitable ventures.

Tests and Criticisms of the Financial Repression Approach

The component of the financial repression approach that is easiest to test is the interest rate elasticity of savings. It makes intuitive sense that savers respond to the reward for holding financial assets, conditional on the risk of holding these assets. It is questionable, however, whether a complete specification of the model would involve just the rate of interest, as the reward for holding financial assets, and the rate of inflation, as the risk of holding financial assets. In fact, empirical tests of this formulation of the interest rate elasticity hypothesis have yielded ambiguous results, at least for the Philippines. A summary discussion follows.[3]

A number of studies utilized time series data from the national income accounts to test mainly the interest rate and income variables as determinants of personal savings. Van Atta (1971) and Tan (1980) found that real personal income per capita has a significant positive effect on real personal savings per capita, while the real rate of interest has no effect. Burkner (1980) tested the same hypothesis by using a longer time period, 1950-1977, with greater variance since it included years that had effective limits on interest rates charged as well as years in which the usury legislation was not operative. He found that the increase in interest rates, whether nominal or real, had a significant effect on the level of personal savings. Fry (1978) tested a savings function using pooled time series data of seven Asian countries, including the Philippines, 1962-1972, with results supporting the "interest rate elasticity" hypothesis. The study was expanded later to cover more countries and the period 1961-1983 (ADB 1985) confirming Fry's results. These results, however, were reversed by Giovannini (1985) who excluded from the sample the South Korea observations for the years 1967 and 1968 on the grounds that they followed closely the financial reforms of 1965 and as a result represented a whole package, as opposed to a pure liberalization of the rate of interest. In conclusion, one is inclined to agree with Modigliani (1986: 304) that "... despite a hot debate, no convincing general evidence either way has been produced, which leads me to the provisional view that [the savings rate] is largely independent of the interest rate."

As opposed to the paramount emphasis on the rate of interest in the McKinnon-Shaw hypothesis, Patrick (1966) suggested that savings mobilization is severely constrained by the absence of formal financial institutions offering financial assets. Especially in the rural sector of developing countries, the creation of FFI's in advance of the demand for their services is expected to be of crucial importance for mobilization of savings. He formulates, therefore, the "institution-elasticity" approach (or the "supply-leading" approach), which emphasizes accessibility to financial services as a determinant of financial savings.

The hypotheses that emphasize yield and accessibility are just partial features to a "financial instruments" approach suggested by Burkner (1980). Other features of importance to savers are risk, liquidity, information, and product variation. Risk is only partly the rate of inflation emphasized by McKinnon; the risk of bank closures and the availability (and credibility) of a deposit insurance scheme become important. Different instruments, for example, savings deposits versus government bonds, have different liquidity characteristics. Product variation is rather limited in the financial markets of developing countries and specific covenants such as insurance coverage and special credit terms cannot be easily developed. Finally, information includes not only the accessibility of formal financial intermediaries and their terms that should be in a simple, easy-to-compare format, but also the reliability of information in the sense that the rules of the game have certain stability. Financial deregulation, especially in the environment of a developing country where competition is limited, may result in disinformation through frequent and confusing signal changes. The situation in the United States with the recent wave of deregulation (airlines, telephone, banks) is fastly approaching this level — despite the huge size of the market and the existence of credible competition.

The New Institutional Economics Approach
While the new institutional economics adheres to the importance of

markets, it does not necessarily subscribe to the notion that perfect markets are a law of nature, the result of mutually offsetting selfish competitive drives. In imperfect markets, "unitary prices" and equilibrium "market clearing prices" are not a logical necessity either. Transaction costs exist and are incorporated in market prices which vary depending on the behavior of market agents. Market auctions, moreover, are often ineffective due to difficulties in specifying and monitoring the other agent's actions. Contracting parties, as a result, are compelled to make use of non-price strategies such as quantity rationing and market interlinkage. As Williamson (1987: 585-86) noted:

> Institutional economics ... maintains that economic institutions matter....
> [They] are important not merely as technological entities but also as governmental structures. This latter conception brings in the information processing and the incentive and control differences of alternative economic modes of organization.... [The new institutional economics is also] cognizant that the central problems of economic organizations are attributable to the *behavioral attributes* of human actors. Behavioral assumptions are thus regarded as an important part of the exercise.

Although there has not been so far a systematic analysis of the credit markets based on the precepts of the new institutional economics, various strands of the modern credit literature build on incentive problems and transaction costs that emerge especially in a contract involving the promise to pay in the future. As already indicated in Chapter 1, such promise involves asymmetry in information between lender and borrower and breeds moral hazard and adverse selection of borrower risk. Trust is the means of overcoming the incentive problems inherent in the nature of the credit contract. In developed countries (DC's) and in formal credit markets trust can be founded on impersonal market mechanisms, such as collateral. In developing countries (LDC's), and especially in informal credit markets, market institutions are not complete and poverty limits the availability of collateral. Other types of restrictive covenants that are less "at arm's length" and more personalistic—from market interlinkage to family ties—become crucial characteristics of the credit contract. The "structural distortions" observed in credit markets are therefore the result of institutional responses to overcome inherent incentive problems. It follows that the informal credit market becomes an appropriate case study to highlight certain aspects of incentive problems that are emphasized by the new institutional economics, and to connect various "structural distortions" to the form of market organization.

Goods, Services and Economic Rents

Traditional literature associates fragmented markets with the existence of barriers to entry. Market fragmentation creates economic rents, that special interests seek to appropriate and are able to perpetuate under certain conditions. When it comes to credit, this view of the "rent-seeking economy" (Krueger 1974) takes a special form. Market fragmentation and economic rents, according to this view, arise due to government regulation that imposes barriers of entry and couples them with interest rate ceilings. The credit market, as a result, does not clear through price rationing (price closure). The policy recommendation of perfecting the credit market through deregulation and removing the barriers to entry follows.

The new institutional economics, on the other hand, sees fragmented markets and the economic rents they create not as an artifice of government regulation, but rather as a natural outcome of the existence of non-zero transaction costs. These represent costs which are not normally included in the conventional production costs of neoclassical theory: costs of information, negotiation, coordination, monitoring, enforcement, and so on. The origin of transaction costs is partly only the existence of incomplete property rights. It is also due to the existence of alternative norms of economic behavior, alternative types of contracts, and differences in the "architecture" of socioeconomic systems (Thorbecke 1988). Within this context, the approach of the new institutional economics tries to isolate the transaction costs which, when taken into account, explain why an apparent economic rent is not in fact an economic rent, and thus it is not a profit opportunity for a new potential entrant.

There is a correspondence between transaction costs and market fragmentation which goes beyond the market for credit (Yotopoulos 1989). In fact, in the real world there is a continuum between perfect markets and (extremely) fragmented markets. We will call the two extremes of the continuum, respectively, "pure goods" markets and "pure services" markets. Whether a commodity is transacted in a market that is closer to one or the other extreme depends largely on the inherent characteristics of the commodity itself that determine whether an "arm's-length" transaction is possible (pure goods) or a personalistic relationship between the transacting parties is also required (services).

The *differentia specifica* that fixes a point in the continuum between goods and services is *trust* (or reputation). Transactions in goods establish rights over objects and the appropriability of these rights is possible with relatively small transaction costs. Transactions in services, on the other hand, involve the obligation by a party to deliver according to certain specifications. This means that services are usually more "customized" than goods, i.e., their markets are more imperfect. And since normally it is impossible to establish with certainty the intentions of a party to deliver, it also means that services involve some amount of trust. Trust is commonly based on a personalistic relationship, and it becomes an important element in transactions involving uncertainty. It is the element that accounts for the quality of a commodity becoming a function of its price. Trust, in other words, is the crucial ingredient in the price-quality theorem of Chapter 1.

The distinction, therefore, between goods and services amounts to a specification of the property-rights hypothesis in which the level of trust requisite for the transaction determines the specific form of appropriability a transaction conveys and ultimately the economic rents involved. Economic rents, in turn, reflect the degree of the fragmentation of the market.

Credit in the Continuum of Goods and Services

We have so far postulated that credit transactions involve a crucial component of trust that makes for a personalistic relationship between the contracting parties. The lemmas from this postulate include: (1) the need for regulation (including barriers to entry); and (2) the need for credit rationing in the absence of price closure. Quantity rationing in the credit market implies that a lender allocates his credit funds by establishing his own criteria of credit-worthiness — as opposed to charging what the market will bear. These factors become important characteristics of the industry structure whether we deal with the formal or the informal credit sector.

A credit transaction differs in certain important ways from a spot transaction (the purchase of apples), which makes the former closer to a "pure service" transaction as opposed to the latter (the "pure goods" transaction). More specifically (Diaz-Alejandro 1985):

1. In a spot transaction for apples, prices summarize all information relevant to the transacting agents. The issue of trust arises only in a peripheral manner. (Was the orchard sprayed within the last seven days so that the apples might be contaminated with chemical residues?) The credit transaction, on the other hand, involves a promise to repay in the future which may or may not be totally credible. This calls for the evidence of interpersonal trust which can only be partly established by a loan contract and a collateral. Besides, contract enforcement and collateral liquidation involve significant transaction costs and are therefore inefficient. A personalistic relationship becomes necessary to complement the loan contract. Moreover, should trust collapse, the costs extend beyond the two contracting parties: a run on the bank would impose huge externalities, spreading beyond the depositors to the bank. In such cases regulation becomes inevitable.

2. In credit markets, as opposed to markets for apples, the closure rules cannot rely exclusively on market-clearing prices. "Since there is no humanly possible way of devising a full-proof system for finding the intentions of borrowers, lenders are likely to end-up rationing credit i.e., putting a ceiling on what arms-length customers are able to

borrow, irrespective of their willingness to pay higher interest rates" (Diaz-Alejandro 1985: 2). The existence of asymmetric information can lead to adverse selection of risk. By charging "whatever the traffic will bear" in order to clear his market, the lender is likely to filter in mostly the borrowers who have no intentions to repay the loan (Stiglitz and Weiss 1981).

3. Beyond issues of externalities, regulation is required by the structure of assets and liabilities of banks. Unlike the apple vendors who invest their own capital, bankers operate with heavily leveraged assets by lending only a part of their equity, and mainly lending debt capital, their customers' deposits. Moreover, banks that issue credit have their liabilities payable on demand, contrary to the case of the apple vendor but not unlike governments. This imposes certain limits on banks' portfolios, putting a premium on safe and fairly liquid loans. The pretension of liabilities payable on demand, furthermore, presupposes not only the existence of trust, but sets also limits for the accessibility to the bank, for example, a storefront, long working hours, and dependable schedules. It is observed in Pakistan, for example, that while "motorized credit agents" can develop a personalistic relationship and successfully extend small-farmer credit, they are unable to collect deposits. Deposits are only made in a store with "iron doors and marble counter tops."

The new institutional economics approach developed above emphasizes that credit markets are inherently different from spot markets. It follows that they require different (and more sophisticated) infrastructural market institutions in order to operate efficiently. In DC's such infrastructure is readily available, to the extent that it is taken for granted and often not even noticed. The income constraint is not that binding and the capitalization rate of the productive sector is high in relation to LDC's which makes collateral readily available. Information is better and it flows more efficiently, so that "credit references" can be used on top or instead of the collateral. Trust therefore is more readily established. Bank regulations exist and their enforcement is fairly credible. So is the court system, which can be relied upon to enforce the credit contract, albeit not inexpensively. The new institutional economics, as a result, can serve in DC's as an ex post rationalization of what is happening, rather than as a mechanism for explaining "aberrant" behavior. In LDC's, on the other hand, there is a huge institutional vacuum left when it comes to the operation of the credit markets. This vacuum is filled by the informal sector —which explains why informal financial intermediation is so widespread in LDC's.

The Residuality Approach to the Informal Sector

There has been extensive debate in recent years on both the role of the informal sector in economic development and the characteristics that determine its membership. The interest in the informal sector peaked in the 1960s and early 1970s with the increased international concern for equity and employment objectives and the growing realization that the large-scale urban industrialization strategies had failed to solve the problems of underemployment and poverty. Interest in the informal sector has been revived more recently as income growth in developing countries is viewed as leading to a shift out of agriculture while population growth and excessive urbanization call for preventing a shift out of rural areas. The rural informal sector is expected to meet this imbalance.

Several propositions about the informal sector were established by that early literature:

1. The size of the informal sector is significant in LDC's, both from the point of view of generating output and of providing primary or secondary employment for large masses of population.
2. The informal sector is characterized by several features: ease of entry, reliance on indigenous resources, family ownership of enterprises, labor intensive and adapted technology, skills acquired outside the formal school system, and unregulated and competitive markets. In contrast the formal sector has the obverse characteristics (ILO 1972: 2, Peattie 1987).
3. The informal sector engages in a broad range of multifarious and non-homogeneous activities and as such it cannot be readily approached as an issue of public policy. Activities that fall within the rubric of the informal sector are ubiquitous at all levels of economic development: merchandizing activities by street vendors and hawkers, service activities by cobblers or repairmen, petty commodity production and subsistence production activities, credit transactions, artisanal and small scale manufacturing, either on own account or subcontracted by larger and formal sector enterprises.
4. The informal sector is a marginal economic sector, that serves as a temporary holding ground for the marginal worker — keeping the women and children in household production, the unemployed in parasitic activities, the newly arrived migrants at the edge of permanent employment — with low returns and negligible productivity. The marginality approach to the informal sector was incorporated at various levels in neoclassical economic development, such as surplus labor (Lewis 1954) and gravity-type migration models (Todaro 1968). It gave rise to the "Z-good" literature (Hymer and Resnick 1969), which views the informal sector as producing inferior goods with

negative income elasticity of demand. Its output, as a result, is bound to decline in the process of development as the sector releases labor to formal, more productive employment.

In contrast to (4) above, we advance the "residuality" approach to the informal sector: the informal sector exists to fill the gaps left by formal-sector economic activities. The production mode of the formal sector defines the overall structure of the prevailing economic system, and the operational mode of the informal sector is determined by that economic structure. The production mode of the formal sector is predicated on the existence of market institutions: the more perfect the markets, the smoother the operation of the formal sector is. Imperfect markets exist by nurture or by nature, however, due to externally imposed distortions as well as to inherent structural distortions. In a segmented market framework, the returns to externalities become significant. The informal sector thrives by internalizing such externalities. It comes in to fill the vacuum that the institutional constraints to the operation of the formal sector have left.

The Testable Hypotheses

A number of propositions regarding the informal credit sector follows from the approach of the new institutional economics advanced above and these are formulated as testable hypotheses. These hypotheses are briefly presented below. Their elaboration and the respective tests will be discussed in the subsequent chapters of this book.

1. *Identifiable gaps in formal credit allocation bring in the informal credit sector to fill the residual or to capture the spillover effect of formal sector operations.*

    The identification of the credit gap is the crucial part of this proposition. An objective criterion is the presence of formal credit which is clearly restrained in terms of areas of operation. Attempts to expand the coverage of formal credit has only created more distortions in the market and has ended in being abruptly withdrawn, because of non-viability or a change in government policies. In such a situation, the nature of the relationship between the formal and informal sector is complementary; it is benign as opposed to conflicting.

2. *Interlinkage of the credit transaction is prevalent in the informal sector.*

    Interlinkage involves contracting between two parties which relates simultaneously to two or more market exchanges, the transactions being linked in an essential manner. There are two main advantages of market interlinkage. First, in a personalistic relationship based on trust, linking credit to the borrower's behavior in another market, serves as an instrument of increasing information. It increases the lender's opportunity of monitoring the borrower's behavior. Hence, it decreases transaction costs which are related, as noted earlier, to the frequency of transactions and which decrease as a function of time.

Second, the decrease in uncertainty and in transaction costs as a result of market interlinkage of credit reflects on the complementary contract as well. Lenders in general consider the credit-complementary activity, whether farming, trading, rice milling, or input dealership, as their primary economic activity and principal source of income. The risk and uncertainty associated with the regular and reliable supply of inputs for their respective primary economic activities provides an additional motive for interlinking credit. Landlords are uncertain about the level of tenants' effort and are wary of any shirking that may take place reducing their share of the harvest. Traders, including rice-millers and wholesalers, have no assurance regarding their share of the farmers' output that determines their supply of selling inventories. Input dealers are not certain of the level of expected demand for their merchandise. In the absence of developed land markets, rich farmers wishing to have access to additional landholdings, lack prior information on the farmers who are likely to give up their land occupancy or usufruct rights. There is an incentive for these agents to link one market transaction with another, and particularly with credit, if the interlinked contract improves the agents' forecast of the anticipated input supply and therefore their ability to plan ahead.

A wide variety of interlinked contracts arises, therefore, in the informal sector, reflecting both the diverse economic activities in which the market agents are involved and the complexity of their gaming behavior in response to the presence of uncertainty and the individual's limited capacity for acquiring and using information to overcome it. Our survey has identified two main types of informal lenders, trader-lenders and farmer-lenders. Both groups of lenders provide interlinked credit, while the small amount of unlinked credit available is exclusively provided by farmer-lenders.

Five types of interlinkage are distinguished, depending on whether the loan is tied to: (1) the provision of intermediation services in relending and/or procuring output; (2) the sale of output to the lender; (3) the purchase of inputs or lease of farm equipment, i.e., tractor, thresher, etc., from the lender; (4) the transfer of rights over the usufruct of the land to the lender; and (5) the provision of labor services to the lender. The evidence suggests that the first three types are prevalent among trader-lenders, while the last two are prevalent among farmer-lenders. This relationship, however, is somewhat obscured by the existence of a category of trader-lender loans that are tied to intermediation services. These loans represent informal financial layering and create a subcategory of farmer-lenders, the marketing agent lenders. They merit additional comment.

3. *As the scale of moneylending operations expands, financial layering develops for the purpose of maintaining personalistic relationship. This agency relationship is commonly established, which decreases the number of borrowers big lenders can efficiently handle.*

A corollary of the personalistic relationship of informal credit is that the number of contracts that a lender can efficiently handle is rather limited. There are severe diseconomies of scale in monitoring personal behavior and in collecting information. Hence the information costs increase as the number of borrowers increases beyond a certain limit. This becomes evident from the extent of the agency relationship we observe in our survey sample.

A trader-lender entrusts his marketing agents with substantial amounts of capital to relend. This explains why the size of loan tied to intermediation services is significantly greater than the size of any other linked loan. Financial layering becomes an empirical implication of the personalistic relationship of informal credit since it reduces the borrowers served by a lender to a manageable number that can be observed closely and known well. Trader-lenders, therefore, who have substantial amounts of money capital and have the scale of operations that involves large inventory turnover, resort to this agency relationship by engaging selected farmers who act as their agents in lending out money and accepting the repayment in kind at the time of harvest, and who also act on their own account as farmer-lenders by tying the loan to the transfer of land rights when the opportunity arises.

4. *Interest rates charged reflect the transaction costs of lending as determined by the character of the personalistic relationship established between the parties.*

Specifically, we expect market interlinkage to have a negative effect on nominal interest charges as it reduces moral hazard and the risk premium which is incorporated in the rate of interest. The interdependence of credit and other market transactions, however, makes the determination of the effective returns to lending more complex. With interlinked markets, the determination of the effective returns to lending, or the real cost of borrowing, takes on several forms, putting the notion of interest in a different perspective. A more comprehensive approach to the measurement of the former is utilized to include implicit charges, for example, input overpricing and output underpricing.

5. *Quantity rationing implies the existence of sorting rules that replace the automatic allocation of the price-closure model.*

An important consequence of the highly personalistic transaction in the informal credit sector is quantity rationing. The quantity-closure rules are modeled and tested for two types of informal lenders in the agricultural sector of the Philippines, the trader-lenders and the farmer-lenders. Specifically, we show that the maximizing objective of each type of lender largely determines their borrower preferences as reflected in the credit terms they stipulate. Trader-lenders, for instance, want to maximize their trading profits while farmer-lenders want to acquire more land for production purposes. The particularity of trading activity and of the process of land acquisition under conditions of inadequately developed land market lead not only to the adoption of selective lending but also to borrower-sorting strategy that is the result of the pattern of competition followed by non-homogeneous lenders. This sorting process is modeled in Chapter 4.

Notes

1. See, for instance, ADB (1985), Burkner (1980), Biggs (1988), Ghate (1986), and Lamberte (1985).

2. Gurley and Shaw (1967) and Kaldor (1963a, b) discuss at length the role of government in increasing savings for capital formation out of domestic sources through taxation.

3. For a review of this literature, see Lamberte and Lim (1987) and Fry (1988, Ch.6).

4. Sah and Stiglitz (1986: 716), who coined the term, define architecture as describing "... how the constituent decision-making units are arranged together in a system, how the decision-making authority and ability is distributed within a system, who gathers what information and who communicates what with whom."

3

Imperfections and Transaction Costs in Credit Markets

The straightforward extension of the new institutional economics in the previous chapter led to the conclusion that credit transactions in general, and especially those in developing countries, are likely to be personalistic, as opposed to arm's-length transactions. Personalized relationships serve an important economic function in societies characterized by social and economic sanctions and conventions (that have nothing to do with standard maximization behavior) and underdeveloped infrastructural environment. Inherent market imperfections relating to limited or missing information, policy distortions, and high transaction costs severely limit the extension of credit in an impersonal fashion and hinder the credit market from clearing at almost any price. These imperfections give rise to various arrangements that serve to substitute for the missing network of complex legal and market institutional infrastructures that are present in more developed countries. Credit rationing, credit layering, and interlinking of markets become necessary features of credit markets in developing countries.[1]

Credit rationing means that the lenders set their own loan approval criteria so that quantity, rather than price closure mechanisms, become appropriate. Credit layering constitutes an intricate lexicographic system of transferring funds. It makes use of special financing arrangements to connect multiple layers of hubs and spokes of lenders and borrowers who are linked together through personalistic ties. Interlinking of markets, which recently has received much attention in the theoretical literature, refers to the linking of two or more market transactions in a contract, with the terms of one being contingent on the terms of the other. These alternative institutional arrangements operate on the basis of personalistic relationships so that the latter define the extent of the informal credit market.

Within this framework, the formal financial sector specializes in the relatively homogeneous market of "prime risks" characterized by well-defined property rights, enforceable formal contracts, and guarantees. The excess demand of unfulfilled credit constitutes a vacuum which the informal sector accommodates. This "residuality" approach implies a complementarity relationship between the formal and informal sector with the latter operating at the qualitative margin of the former. This is a testable proposition that we will examine in the case of the Philippine credit system in this chapter. The findings of several macro and micro credit studies are utilized for the empirical investigation.

Additionally, credit rationing means that there is a limitation of loans contracted with "observationally equivalent" borrowers. This proposition is addressed in Chapters 4 and 5 which deal specifically with the informal sector and examine market interlinkage and the sorting behavior of trader-lenders and farmer-lenders.

Complementarity between the Formal and Informal Credit Sectors

The complementary relationship between the formal and informal credit sectors arises from the fact that the former specializes on the prime or most bankable risks. This manner of operation by the formal sector is in part determined by financial and economic conditions and the stage of financial development in the developing countries (Fry 1988). The narrow accessibility of branches, information collection, and dissemination of financial institutions, as well as the limited ability to mobilize savings and to pool and distribute risks through a variety of products and assets, constrain both the level of funds and the choice of risks of formal financial institutions. This leaves the informal sector to operate in the credit market through quantity adjustments at a multiple interest rate structure.

The nature of the industry, the type of collateral and guarantees available, and the capital base of the borrower are criteria that determine the bankability of a risk. As a result one observes a certain asymmetry in the allocation of formal-sector credit in favor of certain industries and types of loans.[2]

The asymmetrical role of the formal financial intermediation is first evident in the finance that the non-agricultural sector receives in comparison to agricultural credit. Aggregate data in Table 3.1 point to the relatively high proportion of non-agricultural credit to total formal loans and the persistent inadequate credit support to the agricultural sector. Although the agricultural sector contributed an average of 30 percent to GDP for the period 1966-1984, its share of total formal credit was hovering around 8 percent toward the end of the period, down from 17 percent in the mid-1960s. The low share of credit to Philippine agriculture exists despite the fact that there has been a mandatory (25 percent) allocation to agricultural loans imposed upon banks' portfolio since 1975.[3] With the exception of rural banks, the credit portfolio of many other private financial institutions did not meet

TABLE 3.1   Loan Distribution of Formal Financial Institutions by Sector, 1966-1984 (million pesos)

Year	Agricultural Loans		Nonagricultural Loans	
	Volume of Loans	Percent of Total Loans	Volume of Loans	Percent of Total Loans
1966	1,504.3	17.0	73,224.0	83.0
1970	2,851.1	12.5	20,040.3	87.5
1975	7,942.5	6.6	112,525.5	93.4
1980	20,946.4	9.2	206,969.6	90.8
1981	25,376.6	9.1	253,814.3	90.9
1982	27,232.7	8.1	307,030.8	91.9
1983	28,281.1	8.0	323,939.7	92.0
1984	27,070.1	8.1	309,058.9	91.9
Average growth rate				
Current	18.0	23.7		
Constant (1972=100)	3.3	8.4		

Source: Technical Board for Agricultural Credit, *Agricultural Credit Study,* (Manila: TBAC, 1985), p. 24.

this requirement. It favored, instead, economic activities concentrated in the non-agricultural sector and especially in the urban areas — industrial enterprises, real estate businesses, and other service establishments (Table 3.2). For instance, of the total outstanding loans granted by commercial banks in 1983, the agricultural sector received less than a quarter of total loans granted while the commercial and industrial sectors received the bulk of credit extended. Loans extended by thrift banks went largely to real estate while those of specialized government banks went to industrial, financing, insurance, and business service concerns. Only the rural banks which accounted for 4 percent of the total resources of the formal financial system, provided the bulk of their loans (83.2 percent) to agriculture. These agricultural loans were typically extended under subsidized credit programs such as the Masagana-99, Masaganang Maisan, poultry and livestock financing, sugar and coconut, and fishery projects.

Within a sector, the bankability of projects varies widely. Asymmetry in the allocation of formal credit is again observed, with concentration on certain activities and borrower types as shown in the following sections. This leaves a wide credit gap in the non-favored activities and borrowers.

TABLE 3.2   Loans Outstanding of Financial Institutions by Industry as of Year End, 1983 (million pesos)

Industry	Commercial Banks		Thrift Banks		Rural Banks		Specialized[a] Government Banks		Non-bank Financial Institutions	
	Amount	Percent	Amount	Percent	Amount	Percent	Amount	Percent	Amount	Percent
Agriculture, fishery and forestry[b]	23,784.4	21.9	1,608.9	14.9	6,514.9	83.2	4,242.5	12.3	203.5	0.9
Commercial	36,148.8	3.3	1,946.0	18.0	484.6	6.3	1,994.1	5.8	2,631.1	12.2
Industrial	27,369.8	25.2	1,130.7	10.5	226.8	3.0	11,811.5	34.2	6.9	—
Real estate	4,198.4	3.9	3,953.7	36.7	—	—	4,064.2	11.8	5,082.7	23.5
Consumption	2,462.0	2.3	507.8	4.7	—	—	—	1.2	3,654.7	16.9
Others[c]	14,679.6	13.5	1,634.6	15.2	421.7	5.5	12,006.1	34.7	10,040.9	46.5
Total	108,643.0	100.0	10,781.7	100.0	7,648.0	100.0	34,550.2	100.0	21,619.8	100.0

[a]Includes the Development Bank of the Philippines, the Land Bank of the Philippines and the Philippine Amanah Bank.
[b]Includes mining and quarrying.
[c]Includes financing, insurance and business services, and public utilities.

Source: Central Bank, *Twenty-Five Years of Economic and Financial Statistics in the Philippines* (Manila: 1974); Central Bank, *Annual Report* (Manila: 1976, 1980, 1984).

The informal sector operates at the vacuum left at the quality margin of the formal sector.

Asymmetry in Agricultural Credit Allocation

There exists a marked asymmetry within the agricultural sector in the allocation of formal credit that favors the export-crop subsector. Table 3.3 shows that the bulk (44 percent) of the agricultural loans granted in the period 1978-1984 was channeled to export/commercial crops, mostly to sugar (29 percent). Food crops, in contrast, shared 37 percent of total formal loan volume, largely in favor of livestock/poultry (13.7 percent) and rice (7.7 percent), with the balance going to forestry and miscellaneous crops. The volume of credit allocated to the two staple food crops, rice and corn, during the period 1978-1984, has been shrinking continuously, as opposed to the high rates of growth observed for the export and commercial crops, notably coffee, sugar and other non-traditional export crops such as pineapple and bananas (Table 3.3).

The export-crop bias of lending institutions is also evident in Table 3.4 which shows that sugar has the highest loan to output ratio (1.41 pesos for every peso value of produce). Rice and corn, on the other hand, received only 0.15 pesos and 0.04 pesos, respectively, for every peso of gross value added of output. The credit support to sugar seems disproportionately high relative to its share of agricultural output (averaged at 5 percent) compared to rice which held a share of 15.5 percent of the sector's produce for the period 1966-1984.[4]

Size of farm, besides market orientation of the output, also determines the bankability of a loan and is reflected in the asymmetry of credit allocation. A disproportionate amount of formal credit goes to the large farmers, often at the complete exclusion of the small. Table 3.5 shows, for example, that at the height of the Masagana-99 program in 1974, 72 percent of the total volume of formal credit went to farmers with more than 5 hectares of land (Esguerra 1981). Moreover, the Masagana-99 program favored irrigated rice farms, which are generally cultivated by richer farmers (David 1982). More recently, a 1981-1982 Farm Indebtedness Survey found that large farm operators had better access to formal credit than small operators who seemed to have relied more on informal credit sources (TBAC 1986).

Asymmetry in Non-Agricultural Credit Allocation

Even in the urban areas where formal financial institutions tend to be concentrated, non-agricultural credit is allocated in favor of certain businesses and industrial activities and on the basis of size. The household sector and small-scale enterprises are at the qualitative margin of the formal financial intermediation (ISSI 1985).

TABLE 3.3   Agricultural Loans by Commodity, 1978-1984 (million pesos at current prices)

| Commodity | Amount | Total Agricultural Loans | |
		Average Distribution (percent)	Compounded Annual Growth Rate (percent)
Food	58,275	37.21	12.2
Rice	11,984	7.65	(7.7)
Corn	1,295	0.03	(1.0)
Sorghum	327	0.21	16.4
Soybeans	188	0.12	16.2
Fruits and vegetables	12,996	8.31	36.9
Livestock	21,481	13.72	14.6
Fisheries	10,004	6.39	13.4
Export crops	68,720	43.88	14.8
Abaca	2,516	1.61	45.2
Coconut	13,059	8.34	1.1
Coffee	2,439	1.56	62.0
Cotton	546	0.35	6.5
Rubber	556	0.35	(6.6)
Sugar	45,722	29.19	14.6
Tobacco	3,207	2.05	19.0
Others	675	0.43	45.9
Forestry	14,311	9.14	18.3
Others	15,295	9.77	14.9
Total	156,615	100.00	13.9

Source: Technical Board for Agricultural Credit, *Agricultural Credit Study* (Manila: TBAC, 1985) p. 24, Annex, Table 12.

TABLE 3.4 Ratio of Loans to Gross Value Added, 1966-1984 (percent)

Commodity	1966	1970	1975	1980	1981	1982	1983	1984	Average 1966-1984
Agricultural crops									
Rice	16.23	19.29	27.94	14.28	13.74	13.28	8.64	4.98	15.40
Corn	2.97	4.19	8.08	3.64	4.45	5.87	2.69	2.30	4.17
Coconut/copra	9.95	16.41	19.86	63.46	92.01	41.24	14.87	10.96	23.40
Sugar	108.19	89.46	89.99	238.92	160.90	271.69	149.80	110.87	141.13
Others	4.87	7.44	5.00	8.93	21.10	16.76	10.24	16.96	11.26
Livestock/poultry	1.22	5.93	21.08	31.20	33.50	33.10	20.45	16.27	20.14
Fishery	4.59	2.92	7.76	7.32	11.13	10.84	11.89	8.21	8.16
Forestry	7.65	10.85	13.47	26.13	32.92	33.16	21.41	27.20	21.13

Source: Technical Board for Agricultural Credit, Agricultural Credit Study (Manila: TBAC, 1985), Annex, Table 8.

TABLE 3.5   Loan Distribution of Masagana-99 Credit Subsidy Program by Farm
Size, 1974

Farm Size (hectares)	Percent of Total Farms[a]	Percent of Total Formal Credit[b]
< 1	14	0
1 - 3	47	19
3 - 5	24	8
> 5	15	72
Total[b]	100	99

[a]Distribution of farms by size was based on the 1971 *Census of Agriculture*.
[b]Figures do not add up to 100 due to rounding.

Source: Presidential Committee on Agricultural Credit, "Financing Agricultural
Development: The Action Program (Agricultural Credit Plan CY 1977- 1982),"
(Manila: 1977), mimeo.

The loan composition of the various types of formal financial intermediaries (FFI's) reflects the asymmetry in credit allocation. Commercial banks
provided the bulk of their loans to manufacturing and commercial or
trading businesses (Table 3.6). Savings banks and non-bank financial institutions, which used to service the urban household sector by providing
housing and consumption loans, have in recent years shifted their sectoral
allocation in favor of construction, financial, and business services (Tables
3.7 and 3.8). A web of interlocking directorates and common stockholders
that operate among the financial intermediaries and business corporations
abates the tendency for asymmetrical credit allocation and further favors
the large size operations. Doherty (1982) who studied interlocking directorates finds that tie-ups among FFI's in the Philippines are common, for
example, the Social Security System (SSS), Land Bank, Union Bank, and
Bancom Development Corporation have interlocking directorates, and
similarly the Rizal Commercial Banking Corporation (RCBC) and China
Banking Corporation (CBC). Interlocking directorates bridge the financial
intermediaries with business corporations as well. Of the top 1000 corporations in the Philippines that were studied from 1977 to 1979, 453 were found
linked with the 32 commercial banks through 1,132 interlocking directorates (Doherty 1982: 7-11). Figure 3.1 shows an example of interlocking
directorates — those of the Board of Directors of RCBC and CBC.
    The tight collaboration in interlocking directorates is not only limited to
Philippine businesses and bankers but also involves transnational corpora-

TABLE 3.6 Loans Outstanding of Commercial Banks by Industry, as of Year End, 1960-1983 (million pesos)

Industry	1960		1965		1970		1980		1983	
	Amount	Percent	Amount	Percent	Amount	Percent	Amount	Percent	Amount	Percent
Agriculture	450.1	26.7	1,027.8	21.8	1,714.6	20.4	12,010	15.3	14,790	13.0
Mining	21.7	1.3	32.9	0.7	45.7	0.5	7,334	9.3	13,145	11.6
Manufacturing	547.2	32.4	1,264.4	26.9	1,814.0	21.6	27,053	34.4	35,410	31.1
Construction	20.2	1.2	88.8	1.9	135.5	1.6	2,723	3.5	5,818	5.1
Public utilities	41.4	2.5	126.3	2.7	127.2	1.5	645	0.8	518	0.5
Trade	407.1	24.1	1,655.5	35.2	2,489.6	29.7	11,211	14.3	14,573	12.8
Transport	1.7	—	25.7	0.5	715.4	8.5	1,966	2.5	3,886	3.4
Financial institutions	39.4	2.3	191.5	4.1	445.6	5.3	7,914	10.1	12,886	11.3
Real estate	60.7	3.6	106.0	2.3	348.0	4.1	2,298	2.9	4,145	3.6
Services	36.0	2.1	81.9	1.7	249.9	3.0	4,045	5.1	6,217	5.5
Consumption	60.8	3.6	103.5	2.2	303.3	3.6	1,381	1.8	2,392	2.1
Total	1,686.3	100.0	4,704.3	100.0	8,388.8	100.0	78,580	100.0	113,780	100.0

Source: Central Bank, Twenty-Five Years of Economic and Financial Statistics in the Philippines, (Manila: 1974); Central Bank, Annual Report (Manila: 1976, 1980, 1984).

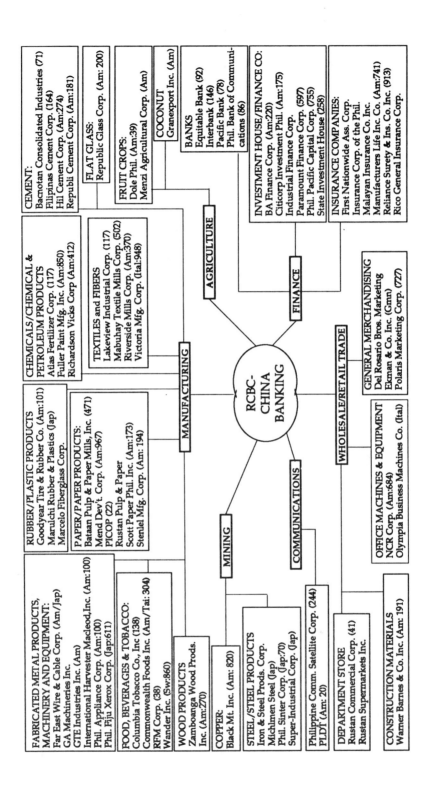

FIGURE 3.1 The Web of Industry and Finance: Intelocking Directorates of the RCBC-China Banking Group with Financial/Industrial Corporations.

The figures in parentheses following each corporation state:
a) Whether there is a foreign tie-up; where there is such, nationalities are indicated as follows: Am (American), Gmn (German), Ital (Italian), Jap (Japanese), and Tai (Taiwanese).
b) If the corporation is among Business Day's Top 1000 in 1981. If so, the number represents the company's gross revenue rank in 1981.

Source: Doherty, John, "Who Controls the Philippine Economy: Some Need Not Try as Hard as Others," Philippine Studies Occasional Paper No. 5, University of Hawaii Center for Asian and Pacific Studies, Honolulu, August 1982.

TABLE 3.7 Loans Outstanding of Savings Banks by Industry, as of Year End, 1960-1983 (million pesos)

Industry	1960		1965		1970		1980		1983	
	Amount	Percent	Amount	Percent	Amount	Percent	Amount	Percent	Amount	Percent
Agriculture	1.7	6.8	6.5	9.8	1.4	1.2	350.7	6.7	234.2	4.4
Mining	—	—	—	—	—	—	5.1	0.1	1.8	—
Manufacturing	—	—	3.4	5.1	1.6	1.4	128.0	2.4	110.4	2.1
Public utilities	—	—	0.05	—	0.08	—	7.5	0.1	0.2	—
Construction	0.1	0.4	0.2	0.3	—	—	569.0	10.9	671.5	12.7
Trade	0.4	1.6	0.05	—	0.08	—	53.6	1.0	108.8	2.0
Transport	—	—	—	—	—	—	64.9	1.2	10.2	0.2
Financial institution	—	—	0.7	1.1	26.6	23.2	1,132.2	21.6	855.8	16.2
Real estate	9.4	37.8	45.4	68.7	78.4	68.3	1,607.0	30.7	1,966.0	37.1
Services	0.1	0.4	0.2	0.3	—	—	335.6	6.4	172.2	3.3
Consumption	13.2	53.0	9.6	14.5	6.7	5.8	988.3	18.9	1,166.7	22.0
Total	24.9	100.0	66.1	100.0	114.9	100.0	5,241.9	100.0	5,297.8	100.0

Source: Central Bank, *Twenty-Five Years of Economic and Financial Statistics in the Philippines,* (Manila: 1974); Central Bank, *Annual Report* (Manila: 1976, 1980, 1984).

TABLE 3.8 Loans Outstanding of Non-Bank Financial Institutions by Industry as of Year End, 1960-1983 (million pesos)

Industry	1960		1965		1970		1975		1980		1983	
	Amount	Percent	Amount	Percent	Amount	Percent	Amount	Percent	Amount	Percent	Amount	Percent
Agriculture	78.5	20.5	86.6	8.4	444.3	11.4	327.7	5.3	434.0	3.3	203.5	0.8
Industry	—	—	—	—	1,122.3	28.8	739.5	12.0	1,750.6	13.3	2,631.1	10.7
Trade	—	—	—	—	66.1	1.7	52.8	0.9	22.7	0.2	6.9	—
Public utilities	—	—	—	—	88.3	2.3	244.0	3.9	394.9	3.0	1,014.7	4.1
Real estate	199.2	51.9	702.6	67.6	1,487.0	38.2	2,579.5	41.8	4,466.7	34.0	5,082.7	20.6
Consumption	105.7	27.6	249.9	24.0	575.2	14.8	1,008.5	16.3	2,352.8	17.9	6,654.7	27.0
Others[a]	—	—	—	—	110.2	2.8	1,220.9	19.8	3,723.9	28.3	9,026.2	36.7
Total	383.4	100.0	1,039.1	100.0	3,893.4	100.0	6,172.9	100.0	13,145.6	100.0	24,619.8	100.0

[a]Includes construction, financial institutions, services and other loan types.

Source: Central Bank, Twenty-Five Years of Economic and Financial Statistics in the Philippines, (Manila: 1974); Central Bank, Annual Report (Manila: 1976, 1980, 1984).

tions and the Philippine government as well. The growth of foreign banks in the Philippines during the 1970s and early 1980s led to the widening of the country's network of financial intermediation. But this did not make it any easier for the smaller borrowers to obtain financing since "for each private Philippine commercial bank, there is an industrial group or foreign enterprise that effectively owns it or dominates its board" (Broad 1988: 173).

The asymmetry in credit allocation is also prevalent among the government-operated non-bank financial institutions. The resources of the Government Service Insurance System (GSIS) and the SSS, unlike the private non-bank financial institutions, are comprised mainly of contributions and premium payments of employees. In the 1960s and early 1970s, more than 80 percent of the loans of GSIS were policy, salary, and housing loans to GSIS members (government employees). But by the late 1970s, GSIS began to phase out housing loans, and loans to its members dropped to only 65 percent in 1980 (IBON Databank 1983). GSIS investments became heavily concentrated in transportation, hotels, manufacturing, and mining (World Bank 1980: 45). In the same manner, SSS expanded its investments in the 1980s in government securities and bonds as well as in direct loans to businesses and direct placements with private commercial banks and financial intermediaries. This has reduced the proportion of loans provided for housing, education, and other services to SSS members (employees of private firms) (SSS 1980).

The Residuality of the Informal Sector

The preceding examination of the credit allocational biases of the FFI's suggests that the role of the informal sector in meeting the loan demands of the rural households, the consumption needs of the urban households, and the capital requirements of many small and medium-scale businesses, including market vending, and retailing, may be quite significant. Both the limited ability of the FFI's to perform their major function of financial intermediation and the endemic asymmetry in formal loan distribution in both agricultural and non-agricultural sectors leave a large vacuum in the credit market. By concentrating on certain "premium" loans, the formal sector leaves the less-qualified loan demand unfulfilled. Thus the residual function of the informal sector arises.

A number of empirical studies have drawn attention to the ability of the informal credit sector in agrarian societies, such as the Philippines, to expand into areas where the formal sector either traditionally does not venture or has curtailed its lending operations for one reason or another. For example, numerous surveys conducted mostly in the rural areas reveal a definite trend for the informal sector to mop up the residual credit demand. The formal credit sources served only a small segment of the rural population; the majority received loans from informal sources (Table 3.9). Agabin *et al.* (1989) indicate that the informal sector also underwrites the credit requirement of the urban areas, but to a lesser extent.

The structure of the informal sector is sufficiently flexible so that it easily adjusts to the changes in the economic and social environment. Dalisay (1937), Kierkvliet (1977), McLennan (1980), and Sacay (1961) observed that historically, smallholder credit in the rural areas was mainly extended by relatives, landlords, traders, or rich farmers. Until the late 1960s, the landlords were the dominant source of loans for the majority of the population living in the rural areas. They usually advanced to their tenants rice for consumption and provided the seeds and tools for cultivation. These were regarded as loans payable, so that at harvest time the landlord's total share included both land rent and interest payment for the loan. Any portion of the tenant's debts that remained unpaid was carried over to the next production cycle.

The surveys conducted during the 1950s and 1960s, as indicated in Table 3.9, reported that the bulk of the loans, measured in terms of total value, originated in the informal sector. Gapud's (1958) survey of 76 Nueva Ecija farmers, mostly share tenants, in 1957-58 indicated that landlords supplied around 61 percent of the loans obtained by the farmer-borrowers. Likewise, the 1961 nationwide survey of farm indebtedness by the Bureau of Census and Statistics (BCS) found that landlords were second in importance to relatives, both in number and loan volume (Table 3.10)

By the late 1970s, however, the composition of the informal lenders had altered as shown in Table 3.10, with the traders and rich farmers replacing the landlords as the major source of loans. This change in the informal lenders' composition can be attributed to several factors. The shift in tenure, i.e., from sharecropping to leasehold arrangements in many areas, has lessened the need for credit as an incentive and monitoring device. The formal declaration of land reform weakened the economic and political sanctions of the landlord, thereby making the existing landlord-tenant relations tenuous. On the other hand, the introduction of new technology in the late 1960s and increased commercialization were largely responsible for the emergence of trader-lenders and rich farmers as the dominant groups of informal lenders.

The overall informal sector's contribution declined briefly in the 1970s with the infusion of massive government credit subsidies to the formal financial institutions with the provision that they be used for extending the reach of agricultural credit. More specifically, the Philippine government introduced in 1973 two agricultural credit subsidy schemes called the Masagana-99 program and the Masaganang Maisan program with the express purpose of modernizing agricultural production and achieving self-sufficiency in rice. During the next few years, the market for formal

TABLE 3.9   Share of Informal Loans to Total Value of Loans, Various Surveys and Years (percent)

Reference Year of Study	Survey Area	Farm Type	Formal	Informal
1950s				
1957-58	N. Ecija	Rice	25	75
1957-58	Nationwide	Rice, tobacco	20	80
1960s				
1960-61	Nationwide	All types, mainly rice	45	55
1966-67	Central Luzon	Rice	57	43
1966-67	Nationwide	Rice	37	63
1968-69	Nationwide	Rice	42	58
1970s				
1970-71	Nationwide	Rice	53	47
1971-72	Nationwide	Rice	46	54
1973	Central Luzon	Rice	64	36
1976	Laguna	Rice	67	31
1976[a]	N. Ecija, Laguna, Camarines Sur, Iloilo, Surigao del Norte	Rice, coconut, others	69	31
1977[a]	N. Ecija, Laguna, Camarines sur, Iloilo, Surigao del Norte	Rice, coconut, others	46	54
1978[a]	N. Ecija, Camarines Sur, Iliolo, Surigao del Norte	Rice, coconut, others	46	54
1978	Bulacan, Camarines Sur, Isabela	Rice	32	68
1980s				
1981-82	Nationwide	All types	62.6[b]	37.4[b]

[a]Study covered 127 farmer-respondents who participated in Bureau of Agricultural Economics (BAECON) daily farm record-keeping project continuously for three years, 1976-1978.

[b]Blow-up of sample of farm indebtedness survey data.

Source: O. J. Sacay, M. H. Agabin, and C. I. Tanchoco, Small Farmer Credit Dilemma, (Manila: Technical Board of Agricultural Credit, 1985), p. 82.

TABLE 3.10   Distribution of Farm Households by Lender Type, Various Surveys (percent)

Lender Type	All Farm Types 1960-61[a] Number of Loans	Amount	Rice Farmers 1978-79 Number of Loans	Amount	All Farm Types 1981-82 Number of Loans	Amount
Landlords	24.4	23.6	20.0	22.4	7.9	6.1
Rice traders	12.7[b]	11.3[b]	26.5	27.2	24.5	31.7
Rice millers	—	—	4.1	2.9	5.4	9.6
Store owners/ other merchants	16.6	20.7	2.6	1.5	4.9	3.9
Input dealers	—	—	12.4	17.6	3.0	3.2
Moneylenders or professional lenders	2.7	3.5	2.0	9.7	—	—
Farmers	—	—	29.8	24.9	17.2	12.0
Relatives	30.1	28.2	c	c	—	—
Friends/neighbors	1.8	1.4	c	c	—	—
Loan associations/ credit nations	0.9	1.9	—	—	—	—
Professional practitioners	—	—	—	—	7.0	7.2
Others	—	—	2.6[d]	2.8[d]	30.1[d]	26.3[e]
Not reported	10.8	9.4	—	—	—	—
Total	100.0	100.0	100.0	115.0[f]	100.0	100.0

[a]Derived from Bureau of Census and Statistics, *PSSII Bulletin*, Series 12, Tables 2 and 12.
[b]Includes corn millers and merchants.
[c]Study did not indicate number nor amount of loan by relation of affinity but reported relations of farmer-borrowers with sources of informal loans, viz., 15.1 percent were relatives, 10.9 percent were neighbors, and 0.4 percent were friends.
[d]Includes construction contractors, handicraftsmen, and professional practitioners.
[e]Mostly nonpalay (e.g., copra and vegetable) commodity traders; also includes overseas workers and informal sources not categorized by economic activity.
[f]Sum of total in the study do not add up to 100.

Source: O. J. Sacay, M. H. Agabin, and C. I. Tanchoco, *Small Farmer Credit Dilemma* (Manila: Technical Board of Agricultural Credit, 1985), Table 5.

credit widened with the massive injection of government loanable funds in the agricultural sector at below-market interest rates. The subsidies were estimated to amount to 359 million pesos.

The introduction of agricultural credit subsidies did not, however, fill up the credit vacuum in the rural areas. In particular, it hardly made an impact on the credit needs of small farmers. The strong bias of the Masagana-99 program structure in favor of large farmers meant that the majority of the farmers could not avail themselves of the credit subsidies (Esguerra 1981). Moreover, Masagana-99 loans, which were restricted for production purposes, usually took the form of cash inputs such as fertilizer and pesticides. A study by Manto and Torres (1974) shows that despite the heavy government subsidies, the informal sector continued to be a significant source of loans even among Masagana-99 recipients.

Both the Masagana-99 and the Masaganang Maisan programs soon became plagued by loan repayment delinquencies that forced the shrinkage of coverage and their eventual phasing-out in 1983. In the Masagana-99 alone, the number of participating farmers plummeted from 531,249 in 1974 to 54,250 in 1980. Correspondingly the share of the formal sector in the rural credit market declined to the level of the 1960s. This meant that farmers who had entered the government programs and had adopted the use of modern inputs, such as seeds and fertilizers, were abruptly left without government credit.

The initiation of the government credit programs in the early 1970s increased the demand for financing modern agricultural technology; the abrupt withdrawal of such credit by the early 1980s only widened the credit vacuum and reinforced the farmers' dependence on informal lenders. The informal sector's credit share increased from one-third in the early 1970s to three-quarters of the total, a level maintained in the 1980s (Table 3.9).

A set of financial reforms was introduced in the early 1980s including the phasing out of most of the special credit programs. In 1984-85, monetary policies became highly contractionary as the country underwent the worst economic crisis in the post-war era. The financial crisis resulted in the closure of some banks and non-bank financial institutions. Agabin *et al.* (1989), Swaminathan (1982), and Serrano (1983) assessed the relative roles of formal and informal lenders in the Philippine rural credit market structure during this period. The picture that emerged unambiguously from both farm-level studies indicates that informal sources were once again dominating the rural market for loans. In fact, the smaller the farmer, the more he relies on informal sources.

Our 1984 survey reached similar conclusions using the data from a purposive sample of 111 rural households engaged in rice and corn production. A schematic diagram of all loan sources in the Survey areas is presented in Figure 3.2. The distinction between marginal and developed areas is made to capture the feature of uneven development in the areas of study. Marginal area refers to the rainfed, low productivity, and less commercialized villages, while the developed area refers to irrigated, high-productivity, and more commercialized villages. In terms of total loan volume granted, Table 3.11 shows that the contribution of the formal sector is insignificant, compared to the share provided by informal lenders. The diminished role of the formal sector in credit allocation is explained by the

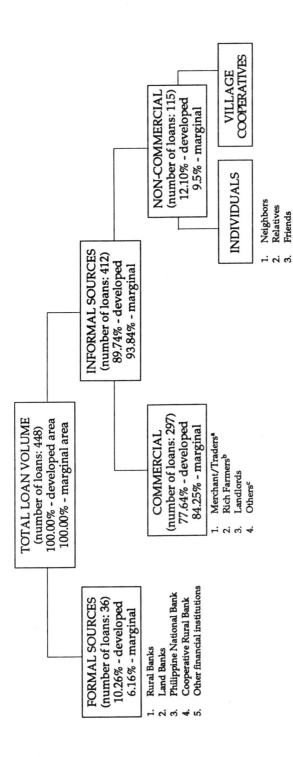

FIGURE 3.2 A Schematic Diagram of all Loan Sources, 111 Farm Households, Wet Season, 1983-84 (in % of total volume of loans per study area)

[a]Merchant/traders category includes agent buyers, miller-buyers, and wholesaler-miller-buyers.
[b]Rich farmers are defined as those cultivating at least 5.0 has. of land.
[c]Others include teachers, local government officials, employees, etc.

Source: Floro, S.L., "Credit Relations and Market Interlinkage in Philippine Agriculture," (Stanford: Stanford University, 1987) Ph.D. Thesis, p.209.

TABLE 3.11 Distribution of Total Loans by Loan Source and Study Area (pesos)

	Marginal Area		Developed Area	
Loan Source	Total Loan Volume	Percent	Total Loan Volume	Percent
Formal lenders	5,141	6.16	98,864	10.26
Informal lenders				
Commercial	184,314	84.25	432,786	77.64
Non-commercial	20,183	9.59	73,185	12.10
All informal	204,497	93.84	505,971	89.74
Total	209,638	100.00	604,835	100.00

TABLE 3.12 Distribution of Informal Loans by Study Area (pesos)

	Marginal Area		Developed Area	
Lender Type	All Household Loans	Percent of Total	All Household Loans	Percent of Total
Noncommercial	20,183	11.25	73,185	14.61
Credit cooperatives	4,147	2.22	22,775	4.55
Relatives/friends	16,036	9.03	50,410	10.06
Commercial[a]	165,458	88.75	427,724	85.39
Traders	66,187	35.50	255,390	50.99
Rich farmers	72,804	39.05	122,431	24.44
Landlords	15,114	8.11	4,504	0.90
Others[b]	11,353	6.09	45,399	9.06
Total	186,641	100.00	500,909	100.00

[a]These exclude informal loans whose lender type category could not be identified. Hence, there is some disparity in the total when comparing with Table 3.11.

[b]These include local government officials, businessmen, employees, schoolteachers, etc.

withdrawal of government subsidies to lending, coupled with the increased submarginal loan demand in the rural areas as economic conditions worsened. Concomitantly, these developments led to the heightened role of the informal sector in filling up the ever widening credit vacuum. Traders and rich farmers, in particular, have provided the majority of informal loans in both the marginal and developed areas (Table 3.12).

The residual function of informal credit in the urban sector paralleled, to a certain extent, its development in the rural sector. The government assumed the leading role in expanding the demand for credit, which was subsequently left unsatisfied thus inviting the expansion of the "traditional" informal lenders such as professional moneylenders and input suppliers, and the growth of non-traditional forms of financial intermediaries such as rotating savings associations, or ROSCAS, pawnshops, moneyshops, and credit unions (Lamberte 1988). In the early 1970s, the Philippine government channeled through the formal sector funds for low-cost housing loans and for financing small and medium-size enterprises. Four government loan funds, namely, the Social Security System Fund, the Development Bank of the Philippines Fund, the Philippine National Bank Fund, and the Industrial Guarantee and Loan Fund, were made exclusively available to government employees and small business entrepreneurs (ISSI 1985). A wide range of formal financial institutions participated as conduits for these funds.

As a result of questionable funds appropriation and high arrearages, a number of credit schemes involving these government funds were suspended in the late 1970s and early 1980s (ISSI 1985: 25-31). In the meantime, rapid urbanization and increasing urban living costs have increased the number of low-income urban households. Small and medium-scale business enterprises, likewise, were being set up in record numbers. They made up nearly 97 percent of the total number of manufacturing establishments in 1980, although they only accounted for 24 percent of the value added in manufacturing (ISSI 1980). Nevertheless, less than 10 percent of small and medium-scale enterprises received credit from private or government banks, let alone financial assistance from the state. This illustrates the importance of the "residual" role of the informal sector in the urban areas as well.

Evidence from anthropological and sociological research touching upon the credit needs and the financing practices of urban households and small enterprises helps illustrate the residual nature of the informal sector. Such studies look mainly into the sources of credit of urban households for food consumption as well as housing (Silverio 1982, Szanton 1972, Davis 1968, ADB 1983), and into the financial needs of small businesses (ISSI 1985, Russell 1985, Keyes and Burcroft 1976, Torres 1984).

For instance, in most urban communities, loans are often incurred because of inadequate income to meet subsistence needs such as food and shelter. These loans often come from non-commercial as well as from commercial informal sources. Non-commercial lenders are credit cooperatives as well as neighbors, relatives, and friends who essentially provide character loans to help the borrower in time of need. Credit provision in this case is part of an income-maintenance scheme that operates in many communities. On the other hand, commercial lenders are individuals who advance loans primarily to earn interest or to help boost their market sales. They are often the local moneylenders, traders, and *sari-sari* (variety) store owners. The latter are particularly noteworthy as a source of credit of urban households since the *sari-sari* store is the most ubiquitous socioeconomic institution in the Philippines (Silverio 1982). Its stock of goods — a combination of items from food market, bazaar, hardware, and drugstore — serves a wide variety of consumption needs of the local community.

The practice of informal financing is no less pervasive among the small, registered and unregistered, business entities, than among the urban households who are commonly depicted as the typical participants in the informal financial sector. Whether these small business entities involve vending, "scrap business," or scavenging, "survival enterprises," or marginal services, the main sources of credit for their working capital are the informal lenders, such as traders, credit unions, dealers, and moneyshops.

The use of informal credit for production purposes is evident in a survey of 79 small, urban-based manufacturers (ISSI 1985: i): "Informal sources were more often considered because they made funds available at a faster rate than formal sources.... Although borrowers repay loans at exorbitant interest rates from informal moneylenders, they still expressed willingness to use their facilities instead of formal banking facilities." Of the total number of respondents, 62 percent obtained credit from both non-commercial as well as commercial informal lenders such as relatives, friends, and local moneylenders.

Finally low-income housing provides an example of the vitality of the informal sector in filling the gaps left from the operations of the formal financial intermediaries. The general disinterest of the formal financial sector in contracting housing loans and the recent phasing out of the government-subsidized housing loans by the GSIS and SSS have exacerbated a serious housing shortfall that already existed in the Philippines. One would have expected low-income families, which constitute 60 percent of the urban population, to be especially affected by the unavailability of housing finance. Nevertheless, the urban poor have built "unconventional" houses without access to conventional financing mechanisms and against the constant threat of demolition and eviction. Keyes and Burcroft (1976) conducted a survey of low-income housing in 1975 with some emphasis on the financing schemes the urban poor have adopted. Among the 51 households surveyed, only a small percentage had access to formal credit for housing purposes: 25 percent of the households obtained government-sponsored housing loans, 8 percent borrowed from a credit union, while the majority of the households (67 percent) availed themselves of loans from friends and relatives.

A more recent study of urban informal credit markets indicates that the share of informal loans received by urban households in 1987 is 45 percent of the total (Lamberte 1988). The role of the informal sector is even more pronounced in low-income urban communities where no formal financial institution operates (Lamberte and Bunda 1988). The growth of self-help institutions such as cooperative credit unions and ROSCAS has been phenomenal, particularly in places of employment and in public markets, where members are fairly homogeneous, know each other, and have regular sources of income. Input suppliers who grant trade credits also seem to rely on personalistic relations, giving loans only to manufacturers directly buying raw materials from them. Even professional moneylenders tend to limit their lending to *"sukis"* or prime clients.

This section has highlighted the asymmetries that exist in the allocation of credit by the formal financial sector and has characterized the role of the informal sector as a residual in closing the gaps left after lending to the "prime risks." It is trivially true that variance in risks and differences in transaction costs are at the foundation of such asymmetries. But to stop at these generalities and to admit that financial institutions respond in this manner does not mean that they perform their resource allocating functions optimally or that the resulting "constrained equilibrium" is efficient or distributionally fair in any meaningful sense. It is also empirically false to assign the cause of asymmetric lending to the existence of interest rate ceilings and other repressive financial policies alone. The growth of the financial system in any country, and its structural features, is in part shaped by the level of economic development and its market infrastructure, and in part by the prevailing network of social conventions that determine the framework for social and economic interaction. Taking the institutional dimension into account, the argument that the better risks get the credit and that the inferior risks would become observationally equivalent if higher risk premia were charged, errs and not only in that it assumes prices necessarily clear the market. It is also naively wrong in presuming the natural existence of objectively "high" or "inferior" risks which therefore implicitly justify the high returns to lending. That these *a priori* assumptions are incorrect, especially in the credit market, is examined below in connection with the loan limitations on observationally equivalent borrowers.

The Personalistic Relationship of Informal Credit

By concentrating on bankable risks, the formal sector deals in relatively homogeneous transactions. Among other things, the existence of collateral and enforceable guarantees in the formal sector capital markets result in observational equivalence in loans with varying risk factors by: (1) partly or fully shifting the risk of loss of the loan principal from the lender to the borrower, and (2) providing those borrowers who have low disutility of default with additional incentive to repay the loans. Collateral becomes a credible instrument of risk-sharing because it is transferable (Binswanger 1982, Floro 1987). Transferability, on the other hand, implies the existence of exclusive and well-defined property rights, along with the legal infrastructure that entails the satisfaction of contracts and enforces a penalty system for their violation, and these may be limited to certain pockets of the economy such as major urban centers (de Alessi 1981, Umbeck 1981).

In cases where property rights are not well-defined, asset transferability becomes problematic, and the collateral required by formal credit institutions is unacceptable. We then have the case of a "missing market" and a "non-viable" credit contract, according to the terminology of the implicit contract theories (Bull 1983: 666). This is precisely the case in many developing countries where poverty makes the availability of collateral rare, and ill-defined property rights and underdeveloped legal infrastructure make the acceptability of the collateral questionable. Usufruct, rather than ownership rights are more prevalent in many developing countries, and they entail only that the tangible resources in question are put into productive use. Usufruct rights, while giving the claimant access to the fruits of the land, do not constitute collateral acceptable to the formal sector. A large component of credit takes place, as a result, in imperfect markets in developing countries (Jagannathan 1987).

The importance of prevailing social and political institutions cannot be underestimated. The existence of paternalism in Philippine banking management, the pervasiveness of interlocking directorates, and the close entwinement of big business, finance, and the state created a so-called triple alliance whose interests dominate major loan and investment decisions, thus favoring certain types of borrowers over others. This further suggests that the straight application of competitive market analysis may be inappropriate even for the formal credit sector.

The personalistic relationship that underlies informal credit substitutes to a large extent for collateral. The historically developed ties on which the personalistic relationship is built offset, to a certain extent, the asymmetry of information and the moral hazard that are both inherent in a transaction that involves a promise to pay in the future in an imperfect market environment.

A familial relationship among relatives and friends often serves as a foundation for extending informal credit. The extended family and kinship institutions forge strong personal trust that allow for high degree of social action and cooperation (Hayami and Kikuchi 1982: 12-16). Frequent socialization and the reciprocal nature of relationships establish the requisite trust within the community or family clan on which credit is founded. It is often given in the form of character loans, which are commonly extended at zero interest rate. However, character loans are relatively limited, and they serve the purpose of collectively providing catastrophic insurance within the context of the extended family system. They largely address cash-flow problems arising in meeting the consumption needs of the household.

In our sample survey, character loans comprise 28 percent of the total number of informal loans (412) received by rural households in both marginal and developed areas (Figure 3.2). Considering that character loans are mostly non-commercial loans, they accounted for only 10 percent and 9 percent of the total volume of informal loans in the sample (Table 3.12). This may be explained by the fact that character loans are often small in size. A shortage of rice for the next day's meal is often met by a no-interest loan, for example, 2-4 kilos of rice, from a sympathetic relative or friend. This type of loan becomes part of the implicit income-maintenance scheme that operates in the community, and thus the question of moral hazard becomes irrelevant. But a character loan of one cavan, equivalent to 44 kilos of rice, without any interest, is very hard to come by. Such a transaction, however, better fits a business contract, and the prohibitive cost of contract enforcement becomes another major concern of the lender.

Transactions that are repeated on a regular basis among the same parties provide another basis for building personalistic relations and lead to credit exchange. The *suki* (regular customer) relationship is prevalent in the Philippines as in other countries (Lamberte and Bunda 1988). It emerges from repeated transactions between buyer and seller, the consumer-household, and shop owners, or market vendors. In von Weizsacker's (1980) terms, buyers extrapolate market relations on the basis of past experience, preferring to return to the same seller as long as the opportunity costs of searching elsewhere are higher. The repeated transactions often build personal ties and feelings of reciprocal obligation, that after some period of time allow for the extension of credit. The regular customer obtains specific advantages from these personalized bonds that include the extension of emergency loans at times of cash-flow crises, or the arrangement of deferred payment schemes on a commercial basis and at a set interest rate. Such advantages often preclude a customer from seeking a better deal, for example, lower prices elsewhere. Both the reluctance of the customer and the deferred payment schemes minimize price competition, facilitate the continuity of repeated sales transactions by the customers, provide quick turnover, and thus solidify the seller's position in the market (Szanton 1972, Silverio 1982).

The lenders' familiarity with the borrowers' economic behavior as a result of transactions in another market constitutes therefore another foundation of the personalistic relationship. At the same time, it limits the domain of credit to a specified small group of individuals who are personally known to the lender.[5] This narrow delimitation of the credit circuit is often overcome by establishing a hierarchical lexicographic relationship between the credit wholesaler and a large number of layers of informal credit intermediaries. This relationship is documented by Russell (1985) in her study of the vegetable-trading system in an upland region in the Philippines. The multi-level supply network of vegetable marketing incorporates a parallel vertical network of credit extension. Russell observed that within a small village of 472 households, there were 19 middlemen who extended credit, or a ratio of almost one middleman for every four vegetable growers in the survey area. What seemed to be a fairly competitive, small-scale informal credit market, under further analysis turned out to be a multi-layered hierarchical relationship based on personalized trade networks. All middlemen were financed by the five vegetable traders who were the buyers for the majority of the vegetable growers. Furthermore, all five of these traders obtained their credit capital from two large Chinese vegetable wholesalers. Ultimately, production loans for 83 percent of the borrowers were extended by the two wholesale agents, by means of a vertical chain of traders, middlemen, and other local intermediaries.

The extent of credit layering (in terms of the number of tiers) has direct allocative efficiency implications for the informal credit sector since it determines the intermediation costs of transferring funds from the original surplus household-saver to the final deficit household-user. As Fry (1988: 280) pointed out, unit resource cost of financial intermediation becomes misleading if there is much financial layering. Credit layering makes each individual lender's costs additive in the total costs of intermediation. While it has been suggested that the aggressive pursuit of selective credit policies has produced extensive financial layering in some Asian countries, including the Philippines, the inherent tendency of informal lenders to adopt selective customer policies on the basis of *ex ante* personalistic ties has produced extensive credit layering in the informal credit markets as well.

Our sample survey offers further evidence of credit layering in the rural areas. The large traders-cum-wholesalers in our sample rarely deal directly with small borrowers and tend to channel their credit through a group of credit-agents who are usually rich farmer-clients. Through their frequent dealings with the traders, both as regular sellers of output and as credit-agents, these rich farmer-clients have established personal trust with the large traders; moreover, they have the assets required for leverage. Most importantly, the rich farmers who act as credit-agents have extensive knowledge about local conditions, such as the time of harvest, and have personal information about the farmer borrowers in their locality, such as their efficiency, level of yields, and other sources of income. Given their locational advantage in obtaining information, these large farmers are usually very effective in disbursing loans, in monitoring farmer-borrowers, and in handling the loan repayment at harvest time. They are known as *mga piyudor*, or "guarantors" of the trader-lenders who do not happen to know personally the small farmer-borrowers.

There are, therefore, two distinct levels of assessment of objective credit risks in our study which favor a credit layering relationship. The large traders can observe the realization of a wider set of loan variables with respect to the rich farmer-clients than other lenders because of their repeated trade transactions with the latter. At the same time, the rich farmers can observe the realization of a wider set of loan variables with respect to the small farmer-borrowers than other lenders not only by virtue of their locational advantage but also due to the common occupation they share — farming. As Ray and Sengupta (1989) point out, these differential risk assessments may lead to a particular type of credit layering — with interlinked loans.

Indirect evidence and partial quantification of credit layering with interlinkage relationship is available from our sample survey. Six of the eight farmer-lender respondents in our sample were recipients of credit capital from either trader-lenders or landlord-lenders (Table 3.13). About 40 percent of the total volume of credit extended by trader-lenders was received by farmer-borrowers who also provided intermediation services by acting as marketing and lending agents (Table 3.14). Moreover, the loans received by these borrowers were significantly larger than the average farmer's loan, the result of the ultimate intent of re-lending, and they were offered at much lower interest rates than other types of loans.[6] These are the characteristics of the agency relationship that exists between the trader-lender and his intermediaries.

The discussion above suggests the existence of an intricate hierarchical system of credit that uses special financing arrangements to tie together in a personalistic relationship the multiple layers of lenders and borrowers. The cascade of credit that flows through this vertical network of personalistic relationships allows the actual number of clients ultimately served by an informal lender to vastly increase.

This chapter has demonstrated that in the absence of market institutional infrastructure and collateral, and given the prevailing social and political institutions that operate within the formal financial sector, the latter does not deliver credit to a large segment of the population. The complementary nature of the relationship between the formal and informal credit sectors

TABLE 3.13   Farmer-Lenders' Sources of Credit Capital by Lender Type and
Study Area

	Marginal Area		Developed Area	
Lender Type	Number of Farmer-Lenders	Percent of Total	Number of Farmer-Lenders	Percent of Total
Trader	2	40	3	100
Large landowner	1	20	–	–
Others[a]	2	40	–	–
Total	5	100	3	100

[a]Others include retained earnings, foreign remittances from abroad, etc.

TABLE 3.14   Distribution of Trader-Lender Loans by Borrower Type and Study
Area (pesos)

Borrower Type	All Household Loans	Percent of Total	Mean Size of Loan	Mean Monthly Interest Rate
Marginal area				
Marketing agents[a]	25,914	39.1	6,957	6.2
Farmer borrowers[b]	40,273	60.8	2,063	16.1
Total	66,187	100.0		
Developed area				
Marketing agents[a]	101,576	39.8	13,500	9.2
Farmer-borrowers[b]	153,814	60.2	3,189	17.3
Total	255,390	100.0		

[a]These are farmers who provide intermediation services to the trader-lender.
[b]Includes both linked and unlinked loans.

arises from the fact that the former specializes on "bankable" and preferred sectors and borrowers, leaving the informal sector to fill in the vacuum. This residual function is accomplished by the informal sector by mainly establishing the requisite trust through various forms of personalistic relationships and the extensive practice of credit-layering. Evidence from our sample survey as well as from other studies illustrate the personalistic character of the credit transactions and the innovative means by which the informal sector internalizes the externalities inherent in the credit market.

Notes

1. This is not to dismiss the presence of credit layering and interlinked markets in developed economies. While they tend to be present in package deals, bank lending, and tie-in sales, these institutional arrangements tend to supplement impersonal market exchanges either as a form of marketing strategy or as an organizational feature of a firm.

2. Similar observations are also made by Biggs (1988) in the case of Taiwan.

3. The mandatory allocation was promulgated by Presidential Decree 717 which required all banks to set aside at least 25 percent of their loanable funds for agricultural credit. The 25 percent quota could also be met by direct agricultural lending to other than agrarian reform beneficiaries and by investment in commercial paper in government securities.

4. The strong sugar bias in formal credit distribution was created by government policies favoring the export crops sector. Such policies were triggered by the favorable export prices in the early 1970s. By 1981, however, the increased popularity of artificial sweeteners and other substitutes reduced the growth of cane sugar demand and concomitantly, brought the world sugar prices down. The Philippines' share of the U.S. quota, moreover, has been steadily declining since 1981 and is expected to disappear within the next three years (APST 1986).

5. The limits of personal supervision and monitoring have also been discussed in various hierarchical models in the industrial organization literature, notably Rosen (1982), and Keren and Lehvari (1983). Williamson (1975), for example, argues that a supervisor can monitor only a limited number of employees so that in large firms supervision must be delegated. Most studies indicate that the quality of monitoring decreases with the span of supervision. Hence, the greater the need for close monitoring, the smaller the group size.

6. Basu (1989) developed a theoretical formulation that demonstrates a direct and inverse relationship between loan size and the rate of interest. The assumption needed to establish such hypothesis is that the loan size reveals the particular borrower's consumption preferences (including the purpose of the loan).

4

A Model of Informal Credit

The previous chapter examined credit as a rationed commodity in the sense that there is quantity, rather than price closure. Quantity rationing in the informal credit market is distinct from other types of quantity closure as it operates in a highly personalistic environment, with the size of loan becoming a distinctly personal attribute. This implies that the lenders set their own criteria for determining the subset of clients they will contract with at a given loan price. The formal sector, to the extent that it concentrates on "prime risks," uses the criterion of the implicit collateral in order to render the loans observationally equivalent. The informal sector is conceded the vast residual loan demand that does not satisfy formal collateral requirements. Thus, informal lenders enlist a personalistic relationship to obviate the adverse selection of risk that a credit transaction may entail.

The assumption of heterogeneity of lenders and borrowers adds another dimension to the ramifications of quantity rationing. Heterogeneity destroys perfect arbitrage in the credit market. Taking the diverse economic considerations of market agents into account, a stronger implication of credit rationing is that certain patterns of competition emerge in the process of lending to observationally equivalent borrowers. These patterns are formulated as testable hypotheses for the informal sector in a model that relates to credit interlinkage and to the sorting of lenders and borrowers. The propositions derived from the model are tested using the Philippine survey data in the following chapter.

Heterogeneity of Market Agents and Credit Interlinkage

The assumption of homogeneous lenders and *ex post* (after acceptable collateral) homogeneous borrowers does service where the formal sector is concerned. It has also been generally employed in most informal sector analyses, notably the information-theoretic, screening, moral hazard/incentive, and surplus extraction models that proliferate in the literature. For example, Bhaduri (1973) and Basu (1984a) examined the credit relationship between landlord-lenders and tenant-borrowers under backward agrarian conditions by postulating that the former are the only credit source for the latter. The same binary distinction is adopted by Braverman and Srinivasan (1981), Braverman and Stiglitz (1982) and Mitra (1983) to name a few.

The multiplicity of credit arrangements observed in developing countries, however, makes such homogeneous-agent models inadequate. A great variety of loan contracts have, for example, been studied in agrarian economies such as Kenya, India, and the Philippines (McLennan 1980, Bliss and Stern 1982, Collier and Lal 1985, TBAC 1981a, Khasnabis and Chakravarty 1982, Timberg and Aiyar 1984, Serrano 1983, Geron 1988, Agabin *et al.* 1989, Bell 1988). Simple loan transactions involving rice coexist with tie-in output loans from trader-lenders and with the more complex land mortgage loans from rich farmers. This is largely a result of the increasing complexity of economies in the throes of transition. Growing specialization and division of labor and the widening network of interdependence lead to dynamic changes in the institutional structures. These dynamics provide considerable scope for dealing with the externalities and high transactions costs associated with informal credit arrangements.

In order to understand the multiple and complex patterns observed in the credit circuit, one has to recognize the fact that market agents are not a homogeneous group. Different types of lenders operate in conditions of agricultural backwardness from those operating in an environment of high productivity and advanced commercialization (Bell 1988). Moreover, there is a continuum between the two situations. The same holds true for the different types of borrowers that exist in the various environments. Nevertheless, the theoretical literature dealing with heterogeneous lenders and borrowers is rather thin, with the exception of Braverman and Guasch (1984), Basu (1987) and particularly Ray and Sengupta (1989). While Braverman and Guasch and Basu incorporated in their models borrower heterogeneity on the basis of different labor productivities and consumption preferences respectively, Ray and Sengupta explored the theoretical implications of two groups of lenders and borrowers as well as the derived patterns of competition.

In reflecting the complexities of Philippine informal credit relations, we introduce a model that allows for heterogeneity of market agents, namely lenders and borrowers. While Ray and Sengupta theoretically examined the conditions necessary for an interlocker (whether trader-lender or landlord-lender) to gain an advantage over the professional moneylender, the model presented below relates the existence of these conditions to the prevailing institutional structures and economic environment in which the informal lenders operate. The diverse characteristics of informal lenders are not therefore arbitrarily assumed; rather they are derived from the specific nature of the economic activities in which the agents are engaged. Specifically, it will be demonstrated that the maximizing objective of each particular group of lenders and the nature of the constraints they face determine their borrower preference and the credit terms they stipulate.

Consonant with the results of our sample survey, we distinguish two types of lenders based on the dominant economic activity they are involved in. The trader-lenders engage primarily in the circulation of goods, i.e., in buying and selling. Wealthy farmers, whether cultivators or merely landowners, also advance credit as farmer-lenders. The conditions that each group of lenders faces in profit maximization are different. Traders, for instance, compete with each other for farmers' output and for a more secure position in the market in an attempt to maximize profits by expanding the inventories they stock and increasing their turnover. In addition, they also have "idle" money capital during certain seasons. We will demonstrate that the combination of idle funds with the need to increase the procurement of farm output leads to trader-lender credit interlinkage. At the same time, trading activity provides an advantage to trader-lenders over the pure moneylenders in the credit nexus. Wealthy farmers, on the other hand, are increasingly faced with the land constraint.[1] The drive to secure more land cannot be easily accommodated within the constrained land markets in developing economies. It is better served indirectly through the debt mechanism. Wealthy farmers, therefore, view moneylending as an important complementary activity that facilitates land acquisition.

Farmer-borrowers are differentiated in the model on the basis of their economic status, as defined by the combination of income, size of landholding, and availability of marketable surplus. Poor borrowers are farmers with low income, small effective landholding, and small marketable surplus. Rich borrowers, on the other hand, have a combination of high income, large landholdings, and correspondingly large marketable surplus. These characteristics alone, however, do not fully determine the degree of risk. Creditworthiness as defined in the credit literature is usually associated with individual traits or with (involuntary) default propensities of the borrowers. Our model will show that, far from being a given borrower attribute, the concept of creditworthiness is jointly determined by the willingness and ability of borrowers to offer certain credit terms, i. e., type of collateral and the acceptability and desirability of such terms to certain types of lenders. The sorting between lenders and borrowers precisely involves this process.

A Trader-Lender Model with Market Interlinkage

Moneylending is a subsidiary activity that complements the trader-lender's primary economic function.[2] It complements trading in at least three ways: it is used to expand the trader's share of the market; it provides an alternative use for operating capital during seasonal fluctuations; it is used to reduce the procurement price of output by locking-in a low price or by fixing a harvest-delivery date when the seasonal price troughs occur. These advantages of linking money-lending to trading assure trader-lenders of better terms in their primary activity. At the same time, they ensure clear dominance in the credit market over unlinked moneylending (Ray and Sengupta 1989). They will feature prominently in the discussion that follows.

Trading is an economic activity that is characterized by economies of scale, since the variable operating costs are low relative to the fixed over-head costs, such as trucks, warehouses, or mills. This feature intensifies the competition among traders for market share. Market share can be expanded by increasing the number of farmer-suppliers and/or the proportion of the harvest each one tenders. Price competition is certainly used in attracting more suppliers in other markets. But with regard to trading, a credit tie-in arrangement that can be viewed as a major component of market competition has a distinct advantage. An interlinked credit contract that compels farmers to commit a portion of their marketable output for sale at harvest time becomes a strategic variable in the competitive game since it increases *ex ante* but limits *ex post* competition: after the contract has been signed the borrower who feels dissatisfied, for example, at the stipulated albeit lower procurement price cannot costlessly move to another trader.[3] In drawing the distinction between *ex-ante* and *ex-post* competition in connection to bank credit, Stiglitz and Weiss (1983: 926) notice that this limitation is essential for the intertemporal linkage of contracts and for enforcing long-term commitments.

Intertemporal commitment is especially important since it allows trader-lenders to take advantage of the seasonal fluctuation of agricultural prices and to better cope in competitive environment. Farm prices in the Philippines tend to be lowest when the bulk of wet season production is harvested, and then they begin to rise until a few weeks before the next harvest period (Bouis 1982). This pronounced seasonality of farm prices creates an incentive for the farmer to postpone the sale of his output, if at all possible; and it creates the corresponding advantage for the trader who manages to procure his supplies at the post-harvest, low price.[4]

The interlinkage of credit with the output market enables traders to stipulate harvest time as the date of output sale (which coincides with the time of loan collection). Moreover, as trading operations expand, competition among traders for procurement of goods intensifies. As his distribution network widens, a trader is increasingly compelled to buy output from a greater number of farmers. While such competition usually takes the form of price strategies, traders have found credit provision to be even more effective in assuring the procurement of grains. The advance of cash and/ or inputs, with the stipulation of output sale to the trader-lender, not only attracts more farmers as the trader's future suppliers, but also sets the proportion of the harvest to be marketed as well.[5] Provision of loans becomes an important strategic variable for assuring traders, even before harvest, a share of the grains market. Just as it provides the trader-lenders additional degrees of freedom, credit provision also forecloses the options available to farmer-borrowers and changes the parameters of their utility functions.

The way in which money-lending becomes complementary rather than competitive to the utilization of a trader's capital is portrayed in Figure 4.1. Excluding credit, a trader's working capital consists of money (M) and commodity stocks (C). In anticipation of accumulating inventories, a trader holds most of his operating capital in liquid cash form (M) just before harvest. Right after harvest, the pattern of commodity inventories presents a peak (and of money a trough), and it declines gradually as stocks are liquidated and money is accumulated (M'). Moneylending is an attractive alternative to the (modest) return to demand deposits as long as the loan maturity period can be made to coincide with harvest, when a trader has the maximum need for liquidity. By advancing the loan at the beginning of the production period and by collecting the payment of interest and return of the principal through the in-kind surrender of output, the trader gains a clear edge over other types of lenders. In comparison to the pure money-lender, the trader-lender has the advantage of observing the status of a greater number of variables and he can therefore better fine-tune the conditions of the loan payment on the observed variables. Differential observability exists as the trader maximizes jointly from trading and lending and this amounts to a large extent for the dominance of interlinked over unlinked loans. These characteristics will be formally demonstrated in the trader-lender maximization model.

The trader-lender produces two outputs, trade goods, q_1, and credit, q_2. For the sake of simplicity and without loss of generality, we assume that both outputs are produced with one trader-specific input, capital, which is denoted by x_i. The subscript i takes the value of 1 and 2 indicating physical goods or selling inventories and money capital, respectively. In the case of trade goods, capital input is first transformed into inventories, physical goods, and is thus written as x_1. But whenever physical goods are procured with a tie-in credit arrangement, the notation is x_1^*. Credit, therefore, may or may not be involved in the procurement of physical goods. If it does, we have the case of *interlinked* credit, and the input is then indicated as x_1^*. Both x_1 and x_1^* are assumed to be perfect substitutes. Money capital, on the other hand, enters directly in the production function and is indicated as x_2.

The trader's activities can be expressed by three production functions, all

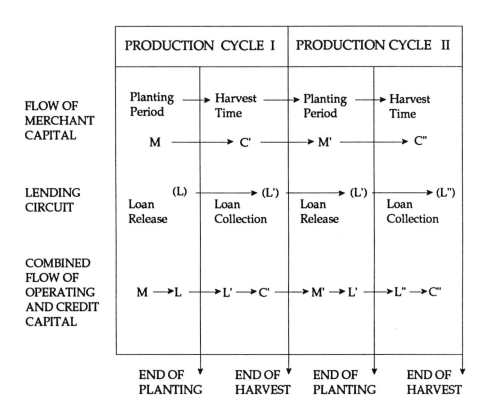

FIGURE 4.1 Schematic Diagram of the Movement of Merchant Capital in Correspondence with the Production Cycle and the Lending Circuit

Variables are defined as:

M = Money form of capital
C = Commodity form of capital
L = Credit capital

strictly separable, with a problem of joint maximization. First, the major activity of the trader is producing trade goods, whether or not they involve credit in their production. The production function of trade goods, q_1, is expressed

$$q_1 = f(x_1 + x_1^*), \quad f' > 0; \quad f'' < 0, \tag{4.1}$$

where the production function f may include milling, drying, and storing on top of the trader's usual transformation services. The arguments x_1 and x_1^* represent, respectively, the inventories that were acquired by the trader without and with tied-in credit.

Second, the trader may utilize his money capital, x_2, for making loans, entirely independently of his trading activities. We write

$$q_2 = g(x_2), \quad g' > 0; \quad g'' = 0, \tag{4.2}$$

where q_2 is credit produced from lending operations with money capital x_2. Loan provision may also involve a tie-in arrangement requiring the sale of goods by the borrower. In this case of interlinkage, we may write explicitly

$$q_2^* = g^*(x_2), \quad g^{*\prime} > 0; \quad g^{*\prime\prime} = 0. \tag{4.3}$$

The functions f, g, and g^* are assumed to be well-behaved, single-valued, continuous functions and with continuous first- and second-order partial derivatives. They are assumed to be concave functions when respective profits are maximized. All values of the input and output levels are nonnegative.

In the absence of market interlinkage, the trader faces exogenously determined prices for both inputs and outputs. The acquisition prices of inventories, r_1, and of loans, r_2, and the prices of their respective outputs, trade goods, p_1, and matured loans, p_2, are fixed at the prevailing market price. By engaging in interlinked trading and lending activities, however, the trader can stipulate both the procurement price of selling inventories, r_1^*, and the price of the linked loan, p_2^*. This opportunity to stipulate the procurement price and price of the linked loan are expressed in symbols as

$$r_1 > r_1^*, \text{ and} \tag{4.4a}$$

$$p_2 \geq p_2^*. \tag{4.4b}$$

That is, the provision of loan, q_2^*, allows for the decrease in procurement price paid by traders for each unit of their selling inventories (grains), r_1^*, below the market price, r_1.

The extent of such reduction depends upon the amount of *linked* loan provided by the trader, q_2, i.e.,

$$r_1^* = k(q_2^*), \quad k' < 0, \quad k'' > 0. \tag{4.5}$$

Note that the decrease in price cannot go on indefinitely. The convexity of the equation, as shown by the sign of the second derivative, means that at some minimum point, any further increase in q_2^* will not allow any reduction in r_1^*. The floor price level would depend upon several factors, such as the nominal interest rate, the demand elasticity of the loan, the extent of competition among traders, as well as availability of alternative sources of credit.

The revenue function is expressed as:

$$R = p_1 q_1 + p_2 q_2 + p_2^* q_2^*, \quad p_2 \ge p_2^*. \tag{4.6}$$

The corresponding cost function is written

$$C = r_1 x_1 + r_1^* x_1^* + r_2 x_2, \tag{4.7}$$

where $r_1 > r_1^*$, and r_2 corresponds to $(1 + r_b)$, where r_b is the borrowing interest rate.

The trader's profit is given by

$$V^T = [p_1 q_1 + p_2 q_2 + p_2^* q_2^*] - [r_1 x_1 + r_1^* x_1^* + r_2 x_2]. \tag{4.8}$$

The interlinkage effect is represented by

$$r_1^* = k(q_2^*), \quad k' < 0, \quad k'' > 0, \tag{4.5}$$

which serves as a constraint in the model. Since the possibility of market interlinkage is allowed, two conditions are added to the profit maximization problem. First, the sum of unlinked and linked loans cannot be greater than the amount of credit capital available:

$$x_2 = q_2 + q_2^*. \tag{4.9}$$

Secondly, and by definition, we assume that

$$\text{if } x_1^* > 0, \quad \text{then } q_2^* > 0, \text{ and}$$

$$\text{if } x_1^* = 0, \quad \text{then } q_2^* = 0. \tag{4.10}$$

This states that the procurement of tied-in physical goods presupposes the existence of tied-in credit. Otherwise, no market interlinkage exists between trading and lending activities.

Substituting (4.1) and (4.9) into (4.8), we get

$$V^T = [p_1 f(x_1 + x_1^*) + p_2 q_2 + p_2^* q_2^*] -$$

$$[r_1 x_1 + r_1^* x_1^* + r_2 (q_2 + q_2^*)]. \tag{4.11}$$

The trader solves the problem:

$$\max V^T$$

$$\text{subject to: } r_1^* = k(q_2^*) ;$$
$$\text{if } x_1^* > 0, \text{ then } q_2^* > 0;$$
$$\text{if } x_1^* = 0, \text{ then } q_2^* = 0;$$

by selecting among the following possible outcomes:

Case (1) $x_1^* = 0$ $q_2^* = 0$ $x_1 > 0$ $q_2 = 0$

Case (2) $x_1^* = 0$ $q_2^* = 0$ $x_1 = 0$ $q_2 > 0$

Case (3) $x_1^* = 0$ $q_2^* = 0$ $x_1 > 0$ $q_2 > 0$

Case (4) $x_1^* > 0$ $q_2^* > 0$ $x_1 = 0$ $q_2 = 0$

Case (5) $x_1^* > 0$ $q_2^* > 0$ $x_1 = 0$ $q_2 > 0$

Case (6) $x_1^* > 0$ $q_2^* > 0$ $x_1 > 0$ $q_2 = 0$.

The first and second cases depict situations whereby the trader specializes in only one activity: trading or lending. Independent marketing and trading activities are found to be desirable in Case 3. The trader involves himself in two activities for portfolio diversification, but he sees no advantage to interlinking them. In Case 4, the trader engages in interlinked activities. The last two cases allow the combination of interlinked and unlinked activities.

The possibility that certain goods (input or output) will not be used or circulated is allowed in our model. We therefore state the trader's problem in Lagrange form:

$$V^T = [p_1 f(x_1 + x_1^*) + p_2 q_2 + p_2^* q_2^*] -$$

$$[r_1 x_1 + r_1^* x_1^* + r_2(q_2 + q_2^*)]$$

$$+ L_1[r_1^* - k(q_2^*)], \tag{4.12}$$

to facilitate the application of the Kuhn-Tucker analysis (Baumol 1976, Intrilligator 1971).

The Kuhn-Tucker conditions for profit maximization are:

(a) $\dfrac{\partial V^T}{\partial x_1^*} = p_1 f' - r_1^* \leq 0$ (f) $x_1 \dfrac{\partial V^T}{\partial x_1} \leq 0$

(b) $\dfrac{\partial V^T}{\partial x_1} = p_1 f' - r_1^* \leq 0$ (g) $x_1^* \dfrac{\partial V^T}{\partial x_1^*} \leq 0$

(c) $\dfrac{\partial V^T}{\partial q_2^*} = p_2^* - r_2 - L_1 k' \leq 0$ (h) $q_2 \dfrac{\partial V^T}{\partial q_2} \leq 0$ (4.13)

(d) $\dfrac{\partial V^T}{\partial q_2} = p_2 - r_2 \leq 0$ (i) $q_2^* \dfrac{\partial V^T}{\partial q_2^*} \leq 0$

(e) $\dfrac{\partial V^T}{\partial L_1} = r_1^* - k(q_2^*) \leq 0$ (j) $L_1 \dfrac{\partial V^T}{\partial L_1} \leq 0$

where $x_1, x_1^*, q_2, q_2^*, L_1 \geq 0$.

By the assumption (4.4a), both conditions (a) and (b) cannot be equal to zero simultaneously. Hence, we try to verify which of the two alternatives is permitted by the Kuhn-Tucker conditions. If equation (b) is equal to zero, then we have $p_1 f' - r_1^* < 0$. On the other hand, if equation (a) is equal to zero, we have $p_1 f' - r_1 > 0$, in which case one of the Kuhn-Tucker conditions is violated. Therefore, we conclude that equation (a) must be negative and (b) is equal to zero, which imply that $x_1^* > 0$ and $x_1 = 0$. Since $x_1^* > 0$, it follows from condition (4.10) that $q_2^* > 0$. Case 2 cannot therefore be the optimal solution. This rules out Cases 1, 2, 3 and 6 altogether.

We know that the trader will procure selling inventories from farmer-borrowers. But is there reason to believe that he will not provide any unlinked credit to other non-farmer-sellers? The prevailing case depends upon the parameter value of the stipulated interest rate, p_2^*, in comparison with the market rate, p_2.

For the interlinkage constraint (4.5) to be binding, equation (e) must be equal to zero and the Lagrangian multiplier, L_1, must be positive. Since k'

is negative, the term $(-L_1k')$ in (c) is positive. The equilibrium relations of (c) and (d) then yield $(p_2^* - L_1k') = p_2$, which means that $p_2^* \leq p_2$. In other words, the stipulated interest rate can be equal to or lower than the market rate. If the trader stipulates p_2^* to be equal to p_2, then equation (d) becomes negative, in which case $q_2 = 0$. This implies that the trader will only provide *linked* credit.

Now consider the situation where the parameter value of p_2^* lies between p_2 and $(p_2 + L_1k')$. Equation (d) is still negative and the optimal value of q_2 is zero.

With the application of the Kuhn-Tucker analysis, our model demonstrates that an optimizing trader will not engage in marketing or lending alone (Cases 1 and 2), nor will he enter into another activity, such as lending, independent of his marketing operations (Case 3). He finds engaging in interlinked lending and trading activities to be optimal (Case 4) since there are additional gains in doing so. These gains are expressed in terms of the reduction in procurement price of farmers' output.

The conclusions reached in our model are quite consistent with the findings of other studies. They support the conclusions reached by Braverman and Stiglitz (1982), Mitra (1983), and Gangopadhyay and Sengupta (1986) that the absence of interlinkage can be Pareto-inferior so that an interlinked loan (with trading) always dominates an unlinked loan.[7] The model findings also demonstrate that the conditions of (1) differential observability and (2) clear advantages to an interlocker in the markets in which he is active proposed by Ray and Sengupta (1989) are satisfied in the case of the trader-lenders.

A Farmer-Lender Model with Market Interlinkage

The inadequate development of land markets in developing countries poses a serious dilemma to wealthy farmers wanting to expand their landholdings since it restricts outright transfers of land ownership via the market mechanism. Indirect land acquisition through the medium of debt is more prevalent. Where there are no institutional strictures against land transfers (for example, legal restrictions on the transferability of land ceded through land reform, or restrictions regarding the minimum land-size) and an efficient cadastral system exists, default on a loan that has land as collateral might lead to transfer of ownership rights.[8] On the other hand, if those conditions are not met, as is the case normally in the Philippines, the land usufruct rights only along with other real assets are offered as collateral. The practice of mortgaging usufruct rights is common with small tenants, especially in periods of economic distress, i.e., prolonged drought, consecutive bad harvests, or personal emergencies. The wealthy farmers, on their part, once the question of legal transferability becomes irrelevant, want access to land not for its resale value nor for land speculation, but for its input-augmenting effects in farming activities that are characterized by economies of scale. As long as usufruct rights can be effectively enforced, land occupancy rights become an imperfect substitute to land ownership rights in areas with poorly developed land markets.

The interlinkage of credit with the land market is considerably more complex and subtle than the interlinkage of credit with output; hence it demands more careful treatment than it is often accorded. In the latter case, the lender has access to output upon maturity of the contract as long as the borrower has not defaulted, for example, by having his crop destroyed or by selling it to another trader. In the land interlinkage case, on the other hand, the expectation of transfer of the land occupancy rights is conditional precisely on the expectation of borrower default. While it does not make the credit transaction entirely riskless, the usufruct rights conditionality makes the farmer-lenders more tolerant of borrowers' risk and explains why farmer-lenders may behave differently from trader-lenders. While the latter would like to avoid default, wealthy farmers may find it to their advantage since non-repayment of loan provides the opportunity for foreclosure of land occupancy rights. Moreover, the process of usufruct rights transfer may not happen in any one loan period; it often results only after several periods of continuous default allowing for debt accumulation within historically developed ties. The complex behavior of wealthy farmers in the credit circuit cannot be therefore adequately captured in any static credit model. Despite these limitations, the possible gains of rich farmers from joint farming and lending activities are illustrated in the profit-maximization model below.

The wealthy farmer produces two outputs, namely, farm goods, q_3 and credit, q_2. Assuming that the level of technology and the quantity of land available are fixed, his primary economic activity, which is the production of farm goods, q_3, involves the use of two variable inputs: labor, x_{31}, and capital goods, x_{32}, with given fixed prices: wage per unit of labor, r_{31}, and the price per unit of capital good, r_{32}. As with trader-lenders, the wealthy farmer utilizes only money capital, x_2, for credit provision and faces a market-determined cost of money capital, r_2. The farmer-lender's activities are thus represented by the following production functions:

$$q_3 = l(x_{31}, x_{32}), \quad l' > 0, \ l'' < 0, \text{and} \quad (4.14)$$

$$q_2 = g(x_2), \quad g' > 0, \ g'' = 0. \quad (4.2)$$

Both g and l are assumed to be well-behaved, single-valued, continuous functions.

The farmer-lender's profit function is written[9]

$$V^F = (p_3q_3 - r_{31}x_{31} - r_{32}x_{32}) + (p_2q_2 - r_2q_2). \qquad (4.15)$$

The presence of uncertainty with regard to loan payment adds a new dimension and makes the concept of collateral relevant. The farmer-lender requires as a necessary condition for credit provision that land usufruct rights be foreclosed in the event of non-repayment. Land-credit market interlinkage is therefore introduced in the profit-maximization model by way of collateral requirement. Defaulting on payment of loans with land mortgage leads to the transfer of land usufruct rights.

For simplicity, any production risk faced by the farmer-lender is ignored so that only loan default risk exists. Moreover, it is assumed for the moment that the interest rate charged by the farmer is what the credit market can bear (or rather what his potential competitors, namely the trader-lenders and pure moneylenders can offer). Given the borrower's propensity to default, d, and the lender's personal valuation of land collateral, C, the rich farmer's expected profit function is

$$E(V^F) = [p_3q_3 - r_{31}x_{31} - r_{32}x_{32}] + (1-d)[p_2q_2 - r_2q_2]$$

$$+ (d)[C - r_2q_2], \qquad (4.16)$$

where $0 \le d \le 1$. This states that the expected total return is the sum of his net return from farming, expected gain from interest payment (in the event of loan repayment), and expected loss from loan default.

In the absence of any collateral requirement, i.e., $C=0$, then the expected returns simply become:

$$E(V^F) = [p_3q_3 - r_{31}x_{31} - r_{32}x_{32}] + (1-d)[p_2q_2 - r_2q_2]$$

$$- (d)[r_2q_2]. \qquad (4.17)$$

In this case, the higher the probability of default, the greater is the reduction in the expected returns. If d is large enough to make the expected loss from loan default greater than the expected gain from interest payment, then the lender may refuse to provide any loan at all.

Since the interest rate is exogenously determined at the market, the lender can only raise the expected net returns from lending by requiring a loan collateral with value $C > 0$.[10] As long as the potential capital loss is positive, there is positive utility loss for the risk-averse borrower in the event of default. If the land collateral has a value greater than the loan amount, then the expected returns from lending are larger in the event of default than with loan repayment.[11]

Collateral requirement normally arises as a result of uncertainty with respect to loan repayment, and it transfers the risk of loss from the lender to the borrower. In the specific case, however, where the object of the collateral, land, is lumpy, piecemeal transfers resulting from default are inefficient, and small loans, in comparison to the collateral value, usually go unsecured or unlinked. This suggests that there exists a minimum floor level of land transfer that becomes a necessary condition for land-inter-linked loans to arise. If this condition is not satisfied, then unlinked loans dominate linked loans from the viewpoint of farmer-lenders.

The borrower, as a result, has an incentive to spread his loan demand among different lenders so that the expected loan repayment to any one lender is either small enough to be paid fully, or small enough not to require any land collateral. The lender, on the other hand, is interested in a loan of a size that warrants sizable land collateral, along with a borrower with diminished capacity to repay (i.e., d closer to 1), so that default implies the transfer of land occupancy rights. One way to achieve this is through a series of defaults on small unsecured loans that are rolled over until they reach the size that warrants linking them to land, and the eventual transfer of the collateral.

An important implication of this model is that the process of land transfer via the debt mechanism is a dynamic one. It spans over several credit cycles and involves a continuous interaction between lenders and borrowers. A series of unlinked lending may therefore transpire within evolving person-alistic relations between farmer-lender and farmer-borrower. The fact that the objective of the farmer-lender to acquire more land is not achieved all at once makes the prevailing power relations not easily discernible. Since his success largely depends upon the growing debt obligations and the dwin-dling repayment ability of the borrower over time, unlinked loans can be offered at generous terms not dissimilar from those of character or non-commercial loans. Such behavior of a commercial lender becomes rational only when its cumulative impact on developing strong personalistic rela-tions between agents is taken into consideration. The historically devel-oped ties preclude the possibility of the borrower to seek loans from other lenders and allow for any defaulted portion of the loan to be rolled over to the next period and to accrue over time. It is only when substantial debt has been accumulated and its magnitude renders the borrower incapable of repaying that land-credit interlinkage actually takes place. The mechanism of default is a process by which borrowers lose their land slowly but surely over time.

Sorting Models

An important consequence of the highly personalistic transaction in the informal credit sector is quantity rationing. Quantity rationing implies that:

(1) lenders allocate credit funds by establishing their own criteria of credit-worthiness, instead of clearing the market by charging what the traffic will bear; and (2) lenders do not lend to all observationally equivalent risks.

In this section the quantity-closure rules are modeled for trader-lenders and farmer-lenders, given their respective profit considerations. The profit maximization model in this study specifies the objective function of trader-lenders as joint maximization in their primary activity, marketing, and their secondary activity, moneylending. The profit maximization model of the farmer-lenders, on the other hand, involves gaining control over the usufruct of land, along with maximizing profits from the secondary activity of moneylending. The divergence in the objective functions between the two types of lenders leads to predictable behavioral differences in an otherwise heterogeneous credit market. The heterogeneity is illustrated through the sorting process of the two types of informal lenders among different types of borrowers and their respective rationing rules among equivalent risks. It is also treated in terms of differences in the effective interest rates that apply to different kinds of loans.

Borrower-Sorting Mechanism of Trader-Lenders

It was pointed out in the previous section that trader-lenders behave so as to maximize their inventories of tradable goods right after harvest by converting all cash and loans directly or indirectly into output. This implies not only interlinking credit with output but also sorting potential borrowers on the basis of their probability of default in repaying the loan and delivering the output. We investigate, therefore, the borrower-preference criteria of trader-lenders and the sorting mechanism they use.

Assume the distinction between two types of borrowers: farmers with small landholdings who are more susceptible to default (poor farmers), and farmers with large landholdings who are deemed less likely to default than poor farmers (rich farmers). That is,

$$d = u(n), \quad u' < 0 \quad \text{and} \quad 0 \leq d \leq 1, \tag{4.18}$$

where d is the borrower's propensity to default, and n is the size of the borrower's landholding.

This assumption is reasonable since rich farmers have relatively more collateral to offer in the form of standing crops than poor farmers. Moreover, rich farmers regularly sell their surplus to the market while the poor farmers hardly sell any of their output beyond what is necessary to pay cash expenses. Furthermore, rich farmers deal more regularly with traders, and the latter presumably have greater access to information about rich farmers, which lessens the default risk. Given the distinction between the two types of borrowers, we examine the effect of risk on the trader-lenders' profits to determine their borrower preference. By dropping unlinked activities and the (*) asterisk for linked activiities in equation (4.12) altogether, the trader-lender's profit is defined as

$$V^T = [p_1 f(x_1) + p_2 q_2] - [r_1 x_1 + r_2 q_2]$$

$$+ L_1 [r_1 - k(q_2)].   \tag{4.19}$$

Risk of default affects the profit function in the following manner:

$$E(V^T) = [p_1 f(x_1) - r_1 x_1] + (1-d)[p_2 q_2 - r_2 q_2]$$

$$-(d)[r_2 q_2] + L_1 [r_1 - k(q_2)].   \tag{4.20}$$

Note that, unlike the farmer-lenders, traders do not require usufruct rights over land as collateral. Although the presence of collateral presumably passes the default risk on to the borrower, trader-lenders would face prohibitive transactions costs in appropriation of the collateral. The value of the collateral to farmer-lenders lies in circumventing the restrictions imposed on the transfer of ownership of land. It fully satisfies the lender who is interested in the land-augmenting effect in production.

Substituting (4.18) into (4.20), expected profit becomes

$$E(V^T) = [p_1 f(x_1) - r_1 x_1] + (1-u(n))[p_2 q_2 - r_2 q_2]$$

$$- u(n)[r_2 q_2] + L_1 [r_1 - k(q_2)].   \tag{4.21}$$

In order to determine the effect of the borrower's resource status on trader-lenders' profits, the first-order derivative of (4.21) with respect to n is computed:

$$\frac{\partial E(V^T)}{\partial n} = -u_n [p_2 q_2 - r_2 q_2] - u_n [r_2 q_2]$$

$$= -u_n [p_2 q_2].   \tag{4.22}$$

Since u_n is negative, (4.22) is strictly positive, which implies that dealing with rich farmers leads to higher expected profits. This result is plausible since rich farmers, with their sizable landholdings, are more likely to have marketable output and therefore decrease the per-unit supervision costs of the trader-lender. They also deal more often with traders, reducing the lender's transaction costs in establishing a personalistic relationship. The profit maximization of trader-lenders thus leads to preference for transacting with rich farmers.

Interest Rate Charges of Trader-Lenders

The importance of non-price terms in credit contracts makes the relevance of interest charges limited in the measurement of effective returns to lending. Nonetheless, interest rates perform to some degree a market signaling role, which still partly determines the real costs of borrowing. The adverse selection of risk has to be taken specifically into account when modeling the interest rates charged. Trader-lenders cannot increase interest rates beyond a certain point to fully offset the risk of a loan without screening in the "risky" borrowers and thus increasing the probability of default, d.

Therefore, beyond a certain level of interest, p_{2m}, an increase in the level of interest charged, p_2, positively affects the probability of default as well. Equation (4.18) is modified to take into account the effect of interest on default:

$$d = u(n, p_2), \quad u_n < 0, \quad u_p > 0, \tag{4.23}$$

subject to $p_2 > p_{2m}$.

The new trader's expected profit function is expressed as:

$$E(V^T) = [p_1 f(x_1) - r_1 x_1] + [1 - u(n, p_2)][p_2 q_2 - r_2 q_2]$$

$$- u(n, p_2)[r_2 q_2] + L_1[r_1 - k(q_2)]. \tag{4.24}$$

For a given level of n, the change in profit level with respect to a change in interest rate is given by

$$\frac{\partial E(V^T)}{\partial p_2} = [-u_p][p_2 q_2 - r_2 q_2] + [1 - u(n, p_2)][q_2]$$

$$- [u_p][r_2 q_2] - [u(n, p_2)][q_2]$$

$$= -[u_p][p_2 q_2] - [2u(n, p_2)][q_2] + [q_2]. \tag{4.25}$$

Note that the sign of equation (4.25) is ambiguous since the first and second terms are negative, while the third term is positive. This suggests that the effect of interest rate on expected profit depends upon the relative strength of the two opposite price effects. Trader-lenders are willing to raise the level of interest to compensate for borrower's risk and to offer loans only if the direct positive price effect on profits is not offset by the indirect negative effect relating to an increase in the probability of default, or

$$q > 2up[p2q2] + 2u(n,p2)[q2]. \tag{4.26}$$

If the reverse is true, then trader-lenders will not provide any loan at all. Default-prone borrowers may therefore be excluded from any loan provision even though they are willing to borrow at higher interest rates.

Sorting Behavior of Farmer-Lenders

The type of borrowers who are deemed risky by trader-lenders, on the other hand, are considered credit-worthy by farmer-lenders. The specific roles of default and land collateral largely explain the preference of farmer-lenders for poor borrowers. A mathematical illustration of the effect of borrower's risk on farmer-lenders' profits is presented below.

First, consider the effect of a change in default propensity on expected profit in the absence of collateral. Taking the partial derivative of (4.17), we have

$$\frac{\partial E(V^F)}{\partial d} = -[p_2 q_2 - r_2 q_2] - [r_2 q_2]$$

$$= -[p_2 q_2]. \tag{4.27}$$

It is clear that equation (4.27) is strictly negative which implies that a higher propensity of default leads to lower expected return. With collateral requirement, however, the effect of default on expected profits becomes ambiguous. Taking now the partial derivative of (4.16) with respect to d,

$$\frac{\partial E(V^F)}{\partial d} = -[p_2 q_2 - r_2 q_2] + [C - r_2 q_2]$$

$$= -[p_2 q_2] + C \tag{4.28}$$

The sign of equation (4.28) depends upon the relation between the value of the collateral, C, and the value of the loan, $[p_2 q_2]$. If C is larger than the loan value, then (4.28) is positive. This means that farmer-lenders benefit more from a defaulted loan than a repaid loan. Lenders would particularly encourage default to take place when the value of land collateral is larger than the loan amount or,

$$\frac{C}{[p_2 q_2]} \geq 1. \tag{4.29}$$

We get the same result when the relation between default propensity and resource status of the borrower is taken into account. Recall in equation (4.23) that the borrower's propensity to default, d, depends upon his land resource level, n, and on the level of interest rate charged, p_2:

$$d = u(n, p_2), \; u_n < 0, \; u_p > 0. \tag{4.23}$$

Substituting this into equation (4.16), we get:

$$E(V^F) = [p_3 q_3 - r_{31} x_{31} - r_{32} x_{32}] + [1-u(n,p_2)][p_2 q_2 - r_2 q_2]$$

$$+ u(n,p_2)[C - r_2 q_2].   \qquad (4.30)$$

A change in expected profits following a change in borrower type is given by

$$\frac{\partial E(V^F)}{\partial n} = -u_n[p_2 q_2 - r_2 q_2] + u_n[C - r_2 q_2]$$

$$= -u_n[p_2 q_2] + u_n[C].   \qquad (4.31)$$

Assuming that the collateral value C is greater than the value of the loan, $(p_2 q_2)$, then the sign of equation (4.31) is negative. This suggests that farmer-lenders prefer lending to poor borrowers than to rich borrowers. It is the borrower's willingness to bear the consequences of default and not the borrower's susceptibility to default that determines a borrower's credit-worthiness to farmer-lenders.

It is easy to see why farmer-lenders find poor farmers attractive credit customers. A poor farmer has at his disposal few resources to meet his subsistence needs. This renders him vulnerable to market fluctuations, especially during periods of distress. Credit then becomes a necessary income supplement not only to meet his production requirements but also his family's consumption needs, such as food, and medical expenses. This makes a substantial portion of his loan demand interest-inelastic, or independent of the terms and conditions attached to the loan. Since poor borrowers have smaller marketable surplus to offer as collateral, they are more willing to offer land instead. While this is less acceptable to trader-lenders, it is consistent with the farmer-lenders' objective function.

The inaccessibility of other loan sources, such as trader-lenders, aggravates the poor farmer's vulnerability and weakens his resistance to land mortgages. Furthermore, the accessibility of poor farmers to a pool of farmer-lenders with competitive terms is also limited, since farmer-lenders prefer dealing with farmers within their immediate vicinity and their own economic sphere of influence, so that in case of default they can enjoy the economies of scale from cultivating land adjoining their properties. If so, the neighborhood effect between rich and poor farmers may contribute to the marginalization of the latter through the instrument of indebtedness.

Interest Rate Charges of Farmer-Lenders

The effect of a change in interest rate on profit is shown by taking the partial derivative of equation (4.30) with respect to p_2:

$$\frac{\partial E(V^F)}{\partial p_2} = -u_p[p_2 q_2 - r_2 q_2] + [1-u(n,p_2)]q_2 + u_p[C - r_2 q_2]$$

$$= -u_p[p_2 q_2] + [1 - u(n,p_2)]q_2 + u_p[C]$$

$$= u_p[C - p_2 q_2] + [1 - u(n,p_2)]q_2. \qquad (4.32)$$

The sign of (4.32) depends upon the relative value of C (as determined by the lender's personal valuation) with respect to the value of the loan. If C is greater than the loan value, then the quantity in (4.32) becomes positive. This suggests that when the default risk is made irrelevant by a collateral clause, farmer-lenders find it in their interest to charge the highest interest rate, as this induces the poor borrower to default. The borrower's propensity to default in this case is no longer a variable involving choice; it is actually induced by the lender. The maximum rate of interest that the farmer-lender can charge is determined by the minimum interest his potential competitors are willing to offer. The fewer competitors he has (or the more isolated the borrower), the higher is his upper bound on interest rate.

In analyzing the process of land transfer via the debt mechanism, it is useful to bear in mind that land-linked loans do not always dominate the choice of credit contracts of farmer-lenders. In most cases, the limited size of a particular loan does not satisfy the condition for land mortgage. Not only will an indebted farmer attempt to avoid defaulting on a loan as much as possible in an attempt to cling to his main source of livelihood. He will try also to spread his credit needs over different credit sources as much as possible to avoid the critical amount that renders land collateral feasible.

But farmer-lenders have a certain latitude in modifying their credit terms to help overcome the borrower's resistance to land mortgage. Lowering the rate of interest charged below the maximum level is especially effective in lulling the poor farmer's defenses. At the same time it serves two purposes for the farmer-lenders: (1) it can induce the farmer to borrow more relative to his capacity to pay; and (2) it also can prevent the borrower from spreading his loan demand over several lenders.[12] The short-run cost in terms of foregone interest earnings is offset within the broader maximization objective of trader-lenders that also includes land acquisition.

Notes

1. The importance of land to wealthy farmers stems from its dual nature as a production input and as an asset with appreciating market value. It is true that the farmers' maximizing behavior involves a considerable number of options and from the short-term efficiency standpoint, adoption of modern inputs may have greater net marginal returns than acquisition of more land. The long-run considerations, however, may deem the latter to be a more desirable option. Market fluctuations and uncertainties over other types of assets enhance the value of land as an asset and as a source of livelihood.

2. One characteristic feature of models on interlinked credit and output market in the extant theoretical literature is the implicit treatment of moneylending as the primary economic activity of traders-lenders (Gangopadhyay and Sengupta 1986, 1987, Bell and Srinivasan 1989). That is, the trader is viewed as the prinicipal who provides credit to the farmer in return for the promise of the latter to sell his harvest to the trader. The question of the primacy of an economic activity in joint production functions is not a trivial one. By accurately treating moneylending as a necessary but supplemental activity to trading, one gets important insights on the behavior of traders and on the terms of credit.

3. Bell and Srinivasan (1989) discussed the exclusivity of credit sources in their model. The denial of access to future credit lends credibility to the lender's threat of painful default consequences. The enforcement of the exclusivity of credit sources requires further that the denial of access to credit is also honored by alternative creditors as well.

4. For example, a study by Abbott (1967) in Colombia showed that the immediate post-harvest price of potatoes is often no more than one-third of that realized later in the season.

5. Chaturvedi (1959) provided evidence of the practice in Asia whereby producers, in order to meet immediate financial obligations, are obliged when prices are low to sell part of their output of subsistence crops that they would have otherwise consumed in the family.

6. Bell and Srinivasan's (1989) market interlinkage model demonstrated the redundancy of charging both a commission rate on crop sale (similar to underpricing of output) and an interest charge on the loan in equilibrium contracts. Moreover, they asserted that the desirability of risk-sharing between risk-neutral agents often leads to commission charges alone. While our model does not directly examine the distribution of returns to lending between the various forms that it may take, it nonetheless assumes that the trader is more than just a (passive) financial intermediary. The interlinking of credit and product contracts and enhances the bargaining position of the trader. These then reduce any desirability of risk-sharing on the part of the lender and raise the possibility of monopoly power in the form of price stipulation.

7. Mitra (1983) developed a model of interlinked land-credit market under moral hazard conditions in which the properties of a Pareto-efficient allocation are derived. Using the Langrangian method and the envelope theorem, Mitra demonstrated that "delinking of credit contracts from output contracts would lead to a reduction in profits without any change in tenant welfare" (Mitra 1983:178). A modified version of the Stackelberg-monopolist model was used by Braverman and

Stiglitz (1982) to prove the optimality of interlinked contracts. They proceeded to demonstrate that the interlinkage increases efficiency by shifting the utility possibility frontier outward. Gangopadhyay and Sengupta (1986) also provided a mathematical proof for market interlinkage. They derived the maximization problem faced by a farmer in two situations: (1) if he borrows from a linked-lender (trader-lender in this case); and (2) if he borrows from a pure money lender. They proceeded to demonstrate that of the two types of lenders, the farmer would opt to borrow from the trader since the "linked lender" charges a lower interest rate as compared to that of the "unlinked lender. This low interest rate offered by the trader is, however, compensated by the low price he pays the farmer-borrower for the output.

8. Binswanger (1982: 42) finds that in areas with poorly developed capital and land markets, land transfers are few and limited mostly to distress sales, especially during periods of prolonged drought or consecutive bad harvests and widespread epidemics. See also Bhaduri (1973, 1977) for an extensive discussion of the poor farmer's valuation of his land that leads to infrequent outright title transfers even where institutional strictures do not exist. Bharadwaj (1985) provides an in-depth look at the nature of land markets in agrarian economies.

9. In the notation that follows credit, q_2, which is an output for the lender, appears with the same notation as an input for the borrower, i.e., $q_2 = x_2$.

10. Is there any basis for C to be greater than the loan value at time of foreclosure? To answer the question, we need to make first the distinction between the process of land acquisition and a simple income maintenance scheme. A rich farmer who lends for income maintenance or non-commercial purposes will not be concerned whether C exceeds the value of the loan or not. His main reason for lending is to help the farmer-borrower meet his present needs. Since collateral requirement is merely a risk-sharing device, then requiring a collateral with the value between zero and the amount of loan can shift a portion of the potential capital loss from the lender to the borrower (Binswanger 1982: 33). The situation is different in the present case of farmer-lenders. They are primarily engaged in moneylending activities for commercial reasons. What motivates them is their desire to accumulate more land so that there is an incentive to require collateral whose value is greater than the loan. As Basu (1984b: 147) argued, "this means that the lender's risk is indeed nonexistent. Default is no longer something which the lender fears."

11. A weaker proposition than that of Basu (1984b) is adopted in this model. At the maximum, C is equal to what the lender would have to pay the farmer as compensation for his loss of livelihood, Y. At the minimum, C is equal to the value of the loan and the lender's personal valuation of the borrower's land. This is equivalent to the expected claim on additional surplus that can be appropriated either through rent or profits for t number of periods, discounted to the present.

12. This is similar to predatory pricing. See Scherer (1980) and Isaac and Smith (1985).

5

An Empirical Analysis of Interlinked Credit

The personalistic relationships that form the foundation of informal credit lead to market interlinkage as an instrument for dealing with the asymmetry of information and for improving contract enforcement. Moreover, the models of profit maximization in interlinked markets presented in Chapter 4 confirm the general tendency of this form of contracting to dominate unlinked credit under certain conditions. The purpose of this chapter is to analyze the extent of market interlinkage in informal credit and to test for the economic implications of linked contracts.

The Rationale for Linked Credit

Market interlinkage involves the process of contracting between two parties that relates two or more market transactions with jointly determined terms of exchange. For instance, landlords rent out land to their tenants and at the same time advance loans in cash or kind (mostly food) that are payable upon harvest. Traders secure a regular and reliable supply of output from farmers whose credit needs they meet in return. Workers have their labor services tied to their employers who provide them with consumption credit.

Most of the microstudies on rural credit confirm that the majority of the informal lenders consider the credit-complementary activity, whether farming, trading, rice milling, or input dealership, as their primary economic activity and principal source of income (TBAC 1981, 1985, Serrano 1983). The risk and uncertainty associated with the regular and reliable supply of inputs for their respective primary economic activities provides an important motive for these market agents to actively engage in money-lending. Once these agents, for various economic considerations, enter the credit circuit, the dynamics of the informal credit sector change drastically. The available instruments in dealing with the prohibitive transaction costs and the significant moral hazard and incentive problems include, among others, the interlinking of contracts.

Under conditions of uncertainty and with market agents who are informational channels of decidedly limited capacity and bounded rationality, market interlinkage serves as an instrument of increasing information. Particularly in areas of growing commercialization with increasing volumes of market transactions, the need for additional information over and above what can be acquired through existing personalistic ties is heightened. Extant market transactions become in themselves another important source of information, and this, as Arrow (1974: 39) has pointed out, has pervasive organizational ramifications. Contracting arrangements with *ex ante* and *ex post* tie-in conditions become important features of market exchanges.

The existence of moral hazard produces an environment that is conducive for market interlinkage. Often analyzed in the context of principal-agent relation, interlinking in this case permits the principal to exercise a greater degree of monitoring and control over the activities of the agent. The essence of control gained by the interlocker varies across existing models. For example, Braverman and Stiglitz (1982) and Braverman and Srinivasan (1981) define control in terms of affecting the performance of the tenant-borrower as a cultivator, which in turn, affects the income of the landlord. In the case of credit, interlinked contracting takes place because it improves the lender's forecast of the individual's behavior, and hence, his ability to judiciously select risks from a pool of potential borrowers. Others like Basu (1984b) view interlinkage as a means to reduce the actual risk of default of the borrower. For instance, the landlord reduces the potential risk to zero by offering loans only to borrowers he can control by virtue of a tenancy or labor contract. A third dimension of the so-called interlocker's advantage refers to power relations. As Bardhan (1989c: 240) pointed out, "the very nature of the rationale for personalized interlinkage ... may at the same time act as formidable barrier to entry for third parties and is thus a source of additional monopoly for the dominant party in such transactions."

The decrease in uncertainty and the increase in control over the behavior of the other party through market interlinkage of credit reflects on the complementary contract as well. Landlords are uncertain about the level of tenants' effort and are wary of any shirking that might reduce their share of the harvest. Traders, including rice-millers and wholesalers, have no assurance regarding their share of the farmers' output that determines their supply of selling inventories. Input dealers are not certain of the level of expected demand for their merchandise. Rich farmers, wishing to expand their area under cultivation, operate in an environment of undeveloped land markets and thus lack prior information about the farmers who are likely suppliers of land occupancy or usufruct rights. There is an incentive for these agents to link one market transaction with another, and particularly with credit, if the interlinked contract improves not only the agents' forecast of the anticipated input supply and therefore their ability to plan ahead, but also secures for them a better position or additional bargaining power in the labor, output, and/or land market.

The Prevalence of Linked Credit

A wide variety of interlinked contracts arises, therefore, in the informal sector, reflecting both the diverse economic activities in which the market agents are involved and the complexity of their gaming behavior in the presence of uncertainty and prevailing institutional structures. Our survey has identified two main types of informal lenders providing either unlinked or linked loans to farmers in the marginal or the developed regions. As Table 5.1 shows, the linked loans dominate the informal credit market in our survey. They account for 79 and 82 percent of the total volume of informal credit advanced in the marginal and the developed areas, respectively.

Five types of interlinkage are distinguished in Table 5.2, depending on whether the loan is tied to: (1) the provision of intermediation services in relending and/or procuring output; (2) the sale of output to the lender; (3) the purchase of inputs or lease of farm equipment from the lender; (4) the transfer of rights over the usufruct of the land to the lender; and (5) the provision of labor services to the lender. The matrix in Table 5.2 clearly indicates that the first three types are prevalent among trader-lenders, while the two last among farmer-lenders. In fact, the matrix would have been almost bi-directional if it were not for the category of trader-lender loans that are tied to intermediation services. Since these loans are a substantial portion of the total trader-loan volume and form a vital link between the two lender types, they merit additional comment.

The trader-lender loans attached to middlemen services represent informal financial layering and create a sub-category of farmer-lenders, the marketing-agent lenders, or *mga piyudor*. These lenders assume dual roles as farmers on their own account and as intermediaries for a trader who entrusts them with substantial amounts of capital to relend. In this dual role, they may link a loan to the transfer of land rights, acting on their own account; and/or they can accept loan repayment in kind at the time of harvest, acting as the trader's agents. Their access to traders' loanable funds explains why the mean size of loan tied to intermediation services is significantly greater than the mean size of any other linked loan. The sizable amount of the loan borrowed also has implications on the level of interest rate charged by the trader as will be demonstrated in the next section. Financial layering becomes an empirical implication of the personalistic relationship of informal credit as discussed in Chapter 3, since it reduces the borrowers served by a lender to a manageable number who can be observed closely and can be known well.

TABLE 5.1 Distribution of Linked and Unlinked Loans by Lender Type, Total and Mean Size (pesos)

Loan Type	Trader-Lenders	Farmer-Lenders	All Informal Lenders[a]
Marginal area			
Unlinked loans			
Total volume	2,981	24,580	35,128
Mean loan size	650	456	538
Percent of total	4.5	33.8	21.2
Linked loans			
Total volume	63,206	48,224	130,330
Mean loan size	1,999	1,976	1,945
Percent of total	95.5	66.2	78.8
All informal loans			
Total volume	66,187	72,804	165,458
Mean loan size	1,985	1,448	1,307
Percent of total	100.0	100.0	100.0
Developed area			
Unlinked loans			
Total volume	—	45,597	75,328
Mean loan size	—	970	1,045
Percent of total	—	37.2	17.6
Linked loans			
Total volume	255,390	76,834	352,369
Mean loan size	3,165	2,883	3,004
Percent of total	100.0	62.7	82.4
All informal loans			
Total volume	255,390	122,434	427,724
Mean loan size	3,165	2,326	2,867
Percent of total	100.0	100.0	100.0

[a]All informal lender loans include loans provided by landlords, businesses, local government officials, school teachers and pure moneylenders as well.

TABLE 5.2 Distribution of Linked Loans by Lender and Linkage Type and by Study Area Total and Mean Size (pesos and percent)

Linkage Type	Trader-Lenders			Farmer-Lenders		
	Total Loan Volume	Mean Loan Size	Percent of Total	Total Loan Volume	Mean Loan Size	Percent of Total
Marginal area						
Intermediation services	25,914	6,957	41.0	—	—	—
Sale of output[a]	36,091	2,103	57.1	7,605	774	15.8
Purchase of inputs[b]	—	—	—	1,180	376	2.4
Both input purchase and output sale	1,162	1,162	1.9	21,293	2,529	44.1
Transfer of land rights	—	—	—	18,000	3,568	37.3
Labor services	—	—	—	145	145	0.3
All linked loans	63,206	1,999	100.0	48,224	1,976	100.0
Developed area						
Intermediation services	101,576	13,500	39.8	—	—	—
Sale of output[a]	142,325	3,247	55.5	32,873	2,717	42.8
Purchase of inputs[b]	—	—	—	2,280	427	3.0
Both input purchase and output sale	9,194	1,129	3.6	10,431	2,563	13.6
Transfer of land rights	2,000	2,000	1.1	28,250	4,628	36.8
Labor services	—	—	—	3,000	1,500	3.9
All linkedloans	255,390	3,165	100.0	76,834	2,883	100.0

[a]Also called "*tampa*" loans.
[b]Includes lease of machinery.

The most prevalent loans provided by trader-lenders and farmer-lenders are those tied to the sale of output, and they are known as *tampa* (Table 5.2). They represent more than 50 percent of all linked loans. The *tampa-lender*, who may be a merchant trader, wholesaler, miller, or middleman-farmer, links credit to his primary activity that is output-related, and is intent to see the loan honored at harvest.[1] He protects himself, therefore, against the fungibility of agricultural credit, which can be easily diverted to consumption purposes, by advancing the loan proceeds upon the "release of irrigation waters" or "with the coming of the monsoon rains," i.e., at an advanced stage of land preparation when the utilization of the loan proceeds (for the purchase, say, of fertilizer) is easily demonstrable. The loan repayment stipulations involve the sale at the time of harvest and at a specified discount (usually at 5-15 percent below the harvest price) of all the marketable output of the borrower to the lender who withholds from the proceeds an amount representing the principal for the loan and the agreed upon interest.

Few loans in our sample are directly linked solely to the purchase of farm inputs (seeds, fertilizer, pesticides, and weedicides) or the rental of machinery services (tractor, thresher) from the lender. These cases also commonly involve the sale of the borrower's output. A variation of this arrangement involves a farmer-input-supplier who provides agricultural inputs as loan in kind and in exchange splits the net harvest equally with the borrower. This practice continues so long as the loan principal remains unpaid and is called *hati-hati* or 50-50. It is essentially the modern-day equivalent of share tenancy.

Loans involving a tie-in with the provision of labor services are not so prevalent in our survey. This is largely due to the enormous increase in the number of landless workers in the last two decades that makes access to labor services, even during peak periods, less problematic.

Farmer-lenders are the main source for the remaining types of loans in our survey. As shown in Table 5.1, farmer-lenders provide quite a significant amount of unlinked credit. The loans are usually small, with average value much smaller than for linked loans. Such credit may be extended in order to accommodate both the timing of the farmer-lender cash flows and the credit needs of the borrower. There is greater flexibility in the contract terms with respect to these loans. In some cases, they are given during the so-called "lean months" or that period prior to harvest when farmers face severe cash flow problems. Since the effective loan period between disbursement and collection time is much shorter, the effective interest charged (in the more orthodox method of interest rate determination) increases sharply.[2] Farmer-lenders are also more willing to roll over any portion of the loan that is defaulted to the next loan period.

Farmer-lender loans tied to land can be relatively complex transactions as they may extend beyond one period of production, which is normally the agricultural year. It is not uncommon that default occurs after a sequence of roll-overs of delinquent tied loans. There are two types of loans linked to land, depending on the amount lent, the economic status of the borrower, and the quality of the land offered in collateral. *Sanglang-patay*, or "dead-mortgages," are offered to the few borrowers who can advance collateral of highly productive soils. During the fixed period of the loan (usually three to five years) the lender enjoys the usufruct rights of the mortgaged land, which he cultivates, or receives an agreed-upon portion of the borrower's harvest from that land. Once the stipulated period is over, the usufruct rights are returned to the borrower and the loan is considered repaid in full, principal and interest. In effect, the present value of the stream of the returns of the land for the specified period is capitalized in the amount of principal plus interest.

More frequent are mortgage transactions with poor borrowers and large loan amounts that are disproportionate to the expected returns from relatively small parcels of low-quality mortgaged land. *Sanglang-buhay*, or "live mortgages," become applicable then that entitle the lender to the usufruct rights on the land for an indefinite period, until principal of the loan is paid in full.[3] In this case, the stream of returns that accrue to the lender from the cultivation of land during the period is considered equivalent to the capitalized value of interest, which also reflects the rate of inflation.

Table 5.2 shows that more than one-third of farmer-lender credit was connected to some type of transfer of usufruct rights over land. The advantage of both types of linked loans extended by farmers lies in circumventing the restrictions imposed on the transfer of ownership of land, which range from high transaction costs to outright prohibition. The transfer of usufruct rights, on the other hand, fully satisfies the lender who is interested in land's input-augmenting effect in production. Moreover, debt accumulation that takes place over several loan cycles and successive defaults may also lead to the eventual transfer of ownership over land.

A final category of loans which is not specifically identified in Table 5.2 is unlinked loans that become tied to land after a series of successive defaults. This supposition is based on the practice among farmer-lenders of rolling over small defaulted loans, presumably until the relative size of the amount outstanding, in comparison to the value of the collateral, warrants the establishment of a live mortgage as described above. Thus, even if the option of interlinking with either land or output is feasible, it may not be the optimal choice of contract. This hypothesis, however, cannot be tested rigorously with the cross section data used in the analysis, since they reflect specific moments in the long-term personalized credit exchange relations that span several production periods. It is further investigated in the analysis of borrower-sorting in Chapter 6.

Interest Charges and Transaction Costs

Traditionally, the informal financial sector has been criticized by policy makers and economists alike on the grounds that it advances high-interest credit that is invariably used to finance consumption expenditure; as a result it reallocates funds away from production thus not contributing to output growth and to agricultural development. The argument is misleading on two counts. First, the issue of the use of proceeds of informal lending has been laid to rest by Wai (1977), among others, who finds that 55 to 60 percent of the demand for non-institutional credit is primarily for production purposes. The evidence discussed earlier provides further support for the hypothesis. Informal credit not only helps meet consumption needs but also provides the bulk of production inputs. The second point refers to the notion that all consumption loans are "unproductive" loans. While it is trivially true that consumption does not directly augment the production level and that certain funds may be "wasted" away on conspicuous habits and lifestyles, there are credit needs that relate directly to the reproduction of labor. It is in this regard that consumption loans become a necessary instrument in the continued subsistence of the laboring population.

The issue of interest rates, on the other hand, remains contentious. The discussion becomes absurdly simplified if one compares informal sector interest rates with controlled rates charged by formal financial intermediaries. Basu (1989) pointed out that the notion of interest rates as used in the credit markets of developed countries is hardly relevant in the context of the informal credit market. The normalization process involved in the calculation of interest rates in the well organized market is reasonable since borrowers are rendered observationally equivalent and interest rates are relatively invariant with respect to loan size and duration. The prevalence of quantity and other non-price closures, as opposed to price closure, in the informal credit markets of developing countries, however, enhances the importance of the non-price terms of the loan contract and requires that loan size, presence of interlinkage, and other characteristics are taken into account. This implies that any direct comparison of formal and informal credit market rates of interest becomes problematic.

If the emphasis is shifted from comparing explicit interest rates between formal and informal lenders to that of comparing the respective cost of borrowing, the discussion becomes more meaningful but the outcome remains questionable. The rationing of all credit, including that from the formal sector, leaves much room for implicit charges associated with establishment or enhancement of personalistic ties such as bribes, entertainment, or the opportunity cost of travel involved in securing credit. A study of rural credit in Bangladesh (Ahmed 1982: 135) found that local moneylenders supplied 84 percent of rural loans and estimated that the gross cost of borrowing averaged 86 percent per year, as compared to 108 percent from commercial banks, when all other costs related to enhancing personalistic relationships are included.

One operational approach to the question of interest charges frequently used in the literature involves their comparison to the transaction costs of the lender. Since many aspects of transaction costs are not observable or even quantifiable, any measurement leaves room for questioning and must be viewed as an analyst's construct. So formulated, the issue remains unsettled in the Philippines. Micro-level farm studies by Gapud (1958) and TBAC (1981, 1985) find evidence of substantial monopoly profits accruing

TABLE 5.3 "Usurious" Interest Charged by Informal Lenders (percent of number of loans)

Criteria	1957-58[a]	1978-79[b]
In excess of legal rate (14 percent)	71.5	72.0
In excess of actual lending cost (22.1 percent)	67.1	67.9
In excess of estimated anticipated cost (36.6 percent)	59.5	57.9
In excess of estimated farmer's borrowing cost with bank (34.0 percent)	62.6[b]	60.0
Loans with interest rate above 75 percent	49.0	32.7

[a]Estimates are based on a sample of 224 fully-paid loans of 76 rice farmers for 1957-58, from Gapud (1959).

[b]Estimates are based on a sample of 1,260 fully-paid loans of 888 farmers for 1978-79, from Technical Board of Agricultural Credit (1981).

Sources:
O.J. Sacay, M. H. Agabin., and C. I. Tanchoco, *Small Farmer Credit Dilemma*, Technical Board of Agricultural Credit (Manila: Technical Board of Agricultural Credit, 1985), p. 89.

J. Gapud, "Financing Lowlands Rice Farming in Selected Barrios of Munoz, Nueva Ecija 1957-58" (Undergraduate Thesis, Los Baños: University of the Philippines, 1959).

Technical Board of Agricultural Credit (TBAC), *A Study of the Informal Rural Financial Markets in Three Selected Provinces in the Philippines* (Manila: Presidential Committee on Agricultural Credit, 1981)

to informal lenders (Table 5.3). Quiñones (1982) and Serrano (1983), on the other hand, distinguish among the transaction costs components due to risk premium, cost of administration, and opportunity cost of capital, and find relatively little incidence of monopoly returns. The high interest rates are mostly due to high risk premium according to Quiñones, while Serrano concludes that informal interest rates are lower than expected and in fact informal loans are often cheaper than formal loans (Tables 5.4 and 5.5). The flexibility of informal lenders in adjusting to the borrowers' cash flow streams and their ability to reduce variable costs of lending through market interlinkage account for the cheapness of informal credit. Another study (TBAC 1981: 25) that explicitly allows for interlinkage in accounting for the components of transaction costs finds excess profits of 33 percent per annum for informal lenders (Table 5.6). These profits accrued by reduction in the risk premium through personalistic relationships that reduced information costs (two-fifths) and by market interlinkage through undervaluation of the borrower's farm produce (one-third).

TABLE 5.4   Transaction Cost and Monopoly Profit Incidence of Informal
Lenders by Study Area, 1978-79[a] (percent)

Study Area	Administrative Cost	Risk Premium	Break-even Interest Rate[b]	Proportion of Loans with Monopoly Profit[c]
Bulacan	1.78	43.62	45.40	24.1
Isabela	4.64	21.41	26.05	52.5
Camarines Sur	5.29	32.34	37.63	26.5

[a]These are estimated from 1978-79 Technical Board of Agricultural Credit sample
of 1,260 fully-paid loans.

[b]This assumes that informal lenders do not take into account a profit component
in determining their interest charges.

[c]This assumes that the critical profit level is zero.

Source: Benjamin R. Quiñones, *Explaining Variations in Interest Rates in Informal
Rural Financial Markets in the Philippines* (Los Baños: University of the Philippines,
1982), Master's thesis.

The new institutional economics approach emphasizes the heterogeneity of economic agents that implies the absence of unitary prices (whether
of the market-clearing type or the rationing equilibrium type) since markets
are severely fragmented. Our calculation of interest charges for specific
categories of loans is made for the express purpose of measuring to some
degree the effective returns to lending and concomitantly the real cost of
borrowing in the informal sector. In our analysis we will address the issue
of heterogeneity of lenders and borrowers by computing interest charges
for each loan category, and we shall discuss the observed interest charges
differentials in connection to the costs specific for each transaction.

Effective Interest Rate on Linked Loans

The effective interest rate applicable for linked loans is estimated by
taking into account the total cost of borrowing, C. This consists of the sum
of: the interest charges applied to the principal (which is the nominal
interest rate, r_c, times the amount of loan advanced, L)[4]; plus the two factors
corresponding to the price differentials, for underpricing output at time t,
and overpricing inputs at time t; plus the value of labor services rendered,
evaluated at the wage rate at time t; minus any transportation costs that

TABLE 5.5 Average Interest Rates by Loan Source and Linkage Type, 1980-81 (percent)

Loan Source	Number of Loans	Average Interest Rate[a]
Formal lenders	6	15
Informal lenders	211	21
Unlinked loans	58	66
Non-commercial Storeowners	8	–
Traditional and variants[b]	17	81
Mortgage[c]	2	19
Linked loans	153	9
Traders	133	10
Employers	20	–
All loans	217	20

[a]The estimation procedure takes into account only the interest component of the effective cost of borrowing, referred in the study as Procedure 1.
[b]The main feature of these loans is the "repayment after harvest" clause.
[c]This type of loan stipulates the provision of asset, usually land, as collateral.

Source: S. R. Serrano, *The Economics of Linking Credit to Other Markets in Camarines Sur, Bicol Region, Philippines* (Los Baños, Philippines: University of the Philippines, 1983), Master's Thesis.

would have been incurred if the transaction for output or input was made with a non-lender. We can write for the cost of borrowing as:

$$C = (r_c L) = [(P_{lq} - P_{mq})Q] + [(P_{lx} - P_{mx})X] + [W] - V, \quad (5.1)$$

and we define

C = the total cost of borrowing upon payment of the loan at time $t+1$;

r_c = the stipulated nominal interest rate at time t;

L = the amount of the principal advanced at time t;

P_{lq} = unit price stipulated by lender at harvest $t+1$ on output q, purchased from household i;

P_{mq} = unit price prevailing at market for output q during harvest $t+1$ time;

Q = quantity of output q sold to lender;

P_{lx} = unit price charged by lender on input x borrowed by household i at time of loan transaction, t;

TABLE 5.6 Transaction Costs and Monopoly Profits by Lender Type, 1978-79 (percent)

	Transaction Costs					Profit Components [a]		
	Administrative Cost (1)	Risk Premium (2)	Sub-Total (1)+(2)= (3)	Opportunity Cost of Capital [b] (4)	Annual Interest Charges (5)	Explicitly Charged (6)	"Hidden" Charges (7)	Total (6)+(7)= (8)
Farmer	3.04	1.55	4.59	15.00	44.83	17.71	7.53	25.24
Input dealer	2.35	3.50	5.85	15.00	16.17	(4.99)	0.31	(4.68)
Landlord	3.66	1.98	5.64	15.00	47.73	18.98	8.11	27.09
Palay trader	3.98	1.67	5.65	15.00	67.03	32.36	14.01	46.37
Rice miller	5.74	4.55	10.29	15.00	14.16	(11.39)	0.26	(11.13)
Storeowner	6.24	3.64	9.88	15.00	69.98	43.38	1.72	45.10
Full-time moneylender	3.56	2.15	5.71	15.00	17.00	(3.76)	0.05	(3.71)
Construction contractor	5.73	3.63	9.36	15.00	37.63	9.30	3.97	13.27
Handicraftsman	1.73	1.57	3.30	15.00	18.90	0.54	0.06	0.60
Professional	2.94	0.72	3.66	15.00	11.78	(6.88)	0.00	(6.88)
Total	4.12	2.97	7.09	15.00	55.53	25.68	7.76	33.44

[a]The numbers in parentheses indicate that the implicit profit component is negative after all transaction costs are substracted from the annual interest charges.

[b]This is based on the average deposit rate of interest of rural banks.

Source: Technical Board of Agricultural Credit, A Study of the Informal Rural Financial Markets in Three Selected Provinces in the Philippines (Manila: Presidential Committee on Agricultural Credit, 1981), Table 58.

P_{mx} = unit price of input x prevailing in the market at time t;

X = quantity of input x borrowed by lender;

W = imputed wage for labor service rendered (measured at the prevailing agricultural daily wage at time $t+1$;

L = number of person-days (at eight hours per person-day) the borrower has spent working for the lender over and above what would be required to pay off the loan; and

V = transportation cost incurred if output or input was sold to/ borrowed from a non-lender dealer.

In the case of the *tampa*-loans, the cost of borrowing, C, is added to the principal, L, and the sum is divided by P_{lq}, the unit price of output stipulated by the lender at time t, to determine the minimum quantity of output, min Q, which must be delivered at harvest time in payment of the loan, or

$$\frac{(L + C)}{P_{lq}} = min \ Q \tag{5.2}$$

Once the cost of borrowing has been determined for the entire period of the loan, the effective rate of interest can be calculated and expressed on a monthly basis,

$$r_a = \frac{C}{mL} \tag{5.3}$$

where

r_a = the effective monthly rate of interest; and

m = the duration of the loan in months.

Adjusting for inflation between the time of loan transaction, t, and loan payment, $t+1$, we get the adjusted monthly rate of interest, r_m,

$$r_m = \frac{r_a}{F} \tag{5.4}$$

where F is equivalent to the average monthly inflation index based on the consumer price index between time t and time $t+1$ (NEDA 1984).

The comparison of stipulated or explicit rate of interest and effective rate of interest for various categories of lenders and loans appears in Table 5.7. As in other cases, we have added to the table the distinction between marginal and developed areas to capture the feature of uneven development in the area of the study. The distinction refers to differences in the conditions of production and the degree of commercialization, with the marginal areas being in general those with unproductive and unirrigated soils, resulting in low yields and small quantities of marketable output.

TABLE 5.7   Stipulated and Effective Monthly Rates of Interest by Loan Type and Study Area (percent)

	Marginal Area		Developed Area	
Type of loan	Stipulated Rate (r_c)	Effective Rate (r_m)	Stipulated Rate (r_c)	Effective Rate (r_m)
Unlinked loans[a]	20.0	19.2	14.6	14.4
Linked loans[a]	12.7	17.7	9.7	16.5
Intermediation services	8.7	9.2	6.3	6.2
Sale of output	11.8	17.0	8.4	15.3
Purchase of inputs[b]	13.5	18.3	19.1	21.1
Both input purchase and output sale	14.4	20.7	12.4	15.2
Transfer of land rights to lender	—	—	—	—
Labor services	13.8	26.1	9.2	31.9

[a]Mean for each loan type is the weighted average interest rate for all loans under each category with size of loan as weight.
[b]Includes lease of machinery.

The following observations are prompted by the findings in Table 5.7. Our calculations show that the effective cost of borrowing in the informal sector ranged from 6.2 percent to 32 percent monthly interest rate in the overall area of our study. Although these figures are relatively high compared to those calculated by TBAC (1981a) for the 1978 period and Serrano (1983) for the 1980-81 period, they are not surprising given the general economic climate at the time our survey was undertaken and the specific production conditions faced by farmers during the 1983-84 cropping season. In the area of our survey, in specific, nearly 25 percent of the cropped land was affected by unfavorable climactic conditions. One of the three survey areas was undergoing its third consecutive year of severe drought, which may partly explain not only the high interest rates but also the relative frequency of land mortgages. In agriculture, the period 1983-84 marked the beginning of the "credit crunch" when the agricultural credit subsidy programs were drastically cut and in the process of being phased-out and the local banking system was besieged by bankrupt financial institutions requiring massive government bail-out. Regarding the general macro-environment, the government, for the first time, declared economic bankruptcy in October 1983 and stopped its foreign debt service payments. Moreover, the Philippines was thrown into political chaos at this time following the assassination of a popular opposition figure, predictably intensifying the capital flight abroad. It was the most serious economic crisis faced by the Philippines since World War II and had the most widespread effects upon people's livelihood. The heightened demand for credit coupled with a rapidly shrinking supply of formal loans made for dynamic institutional changes within the informal sector. The terms of credit including the cost of borrowing generally adapts to the changes in the economic and social environment.

Other interesting points that can be gleaned from Table 5.7 are worth mentioning. Examining the impact of market interlinkage on the interest rate, it can be noted that unlinked loans have in general significantly higher interest rates, whether contractual or effective, than linked loans. Moreover, for both linked and unlinked loans, the nominal interest rate is lower in developed areas and higher in the marginal areas. These trends indicate, in part, the importance of the risk premium: the risk of default is greater in unlinked loans and, other things equal, it is greater in the poorer agricultural areas. The broad domain of control variables available to those offering linked loans entails advantages for the interlocker in terms of informational access and avoidance of default.

The relatively high cost of borrowing unlinked loans may also in part reflect the length of the loan period. Since a substantial portion of these loans is taken out just shortly before harvest time and for short durations, lenders are emboldened to charge higher effective interest rates on account of the revealed inelastic demand for credit by the borrower (Basu 1989).

Considering linked loans and concentrating on the effective interest rate, r_m, which reflects the true cost of borrowing, it is evident that the difference between developed and marginal areas is significantly decreased. This constitutes evidence in favor of the transaction costs hypothesis in explaining the variance in interest rates. Further evidence for the hypothesis is provided by the cost-of-borrowing differential for various types of loans, i.e., the rate of interest after adjustment. Loans linked to the provision of labor services possibly bear the highest transaction costs because of the significant moral hazard problem involved. The high effective rate of interest probably reflects the risk of shirking that the lender faces. Loans linked to providing agent services, on the other hand, have the lowest adjusted interest rate, given the enhanced trust and responsibility that the agent relationship entails. The interest charges on loans tied to the rental of machinery from the lender have a relatively low monthly interest rate of about 10 percent. Loans tied to the purchase of inputs, on the other hand, or the sale of output, have the modal effective interest rates which range from 15 to 21 percent. These findings do not contradict the interest rate formation hypothesis of Basu (1989). The wide variation in loan size associated with the different loan categories follows the pattern of an inverse relationship between loan size and level of interest rate.

The significant difference between nominal and effective interest rates originates largely from the adjustment in the price of output. Underpricing of output in the spot transaction that takes place upon loan payment at $t+1$, relatively early after harvest, is a potent means of transferring surplus from farmers to trader-lenders. How widespread such transfer is appears in Table 5.8 where more than half the households in our survey sold their output to trader-lenders. The government marketing agency, the National Grains Authority (NGA), on the other hand, purchased output directly from only a few households. These results tend to support our hypothesis that when markets are interlinked, the particular lender will do well in enhancing his returns in the principal market.

The analysis of farmer-lender loans linked to land cannot be extended to estimate the effective rate of interest, since a one-period survey cannot provide the information to calculate the capitalized value of the stream of land returns that constitute the payment for the principal and/or interest. The information available nonetheless indicates that loans involving the mortgage of land amount to one-third of the total volume (Table 5.2); the holder of the mortgage is most likely to be a farmer-lender (Table 5.9), not only in the marginal areas, where the bulk of loans tied to land occur, but also in the developed areas where they are less common. Finally, Table 5.10 ranks the inability of a household to meet consumption needs as the primary cause of land mortgage, although special needs also feature, such as investment in human capital in the form of education for children or

TABLE 5.8   Type of Output Buyers by Study Area (percent of households with marketed output)

Type of Output Buyer	Marginal Area	Developed Area
Lender[a]	61	67
Non-lender[b]	34	26
NGA[c]	5	4
Others[d]	—	2
All Types	100	100

[a]Lender-buyers may be trader-lenders (of rice, tobacco, vegetables) or farmer-lenders.

[b]Non-lender buyers may be traders or middlemen who did not provide any loan to the seller.

[c]National Grains Authority (NGA) is the government-owned marketing agency.
[d]Others include relatives, friends, etc.

TABLE 5.9 Distribution of Land Mortgages and Associated Probabilities by Lender Type and Study Area

| | Marginal Area | | Developed Area | |
Lender Type	Number of Mortgages	Probability of Land Mortgaged to Lender Type	Number of Mortgages	Probability of Land Mortgaged to Lender Type
Farmer-lender	11	.6875	7	.7778
Trader-lender	—	—	1	.1111
Non-lender	3	.1875	—	—
Relative	2	.1250	1	.1111
Total	16		9	

TABLE 5.10 Percentage Distribution of Land Mortgages Income by Loan Purpose, Income Class and Study Area (percent of total land mortgages)

| | Marginal area | | | Developed area | | |
Loan purpose	Poor (N=15)	Middle (N=1)	Rich (N=0)	Poor (N=5)	Middle (N=3)	Rich (N=1)
Consumption[a]	63	100	—	43	66	—
Production[b]	—	—	—	14	33	—
Payment of past debts	24	—	—	14	—	—
Others[c]	12	—	—	14	—	100
Total	100	100	—	100	100	100

[a]Consumption includes food and medical expenses, special occasions and education.

[b]Production includes operating farm expenses and purchases of farm equipment.

[c]Others refer to expenses related to application and visa processing for employment abroad.

application and relocation costs for migration abroad. These characteristics of loans linked to the transfer of the usufruct rights of land to the lender may suggest that the likely transfer of land to the lender in a later period may be a more important consideration than interest charges on the loan.

Conclusions on the Rate of Interest

The conclusion from the above analysis is that interest rate determination in informal markets is far more complex than what is usually assumed in the traditional approach which is more applicable in better organized formal markets in DC's. There is no *single* market rate of interest observed in the informal market. Instead there exists a large variety of informal credit arrangements bearing a wide range of effective interest rates. The coexistence of these different levels of interest rates requires a more holistic approach to the study of informal credit relations as suggested by the new institutional economics. In this regard, our method of analyzing the structure of interest rates in the informal sector entails not only taking into account the environment-related and lender-specific risk, but also the other parameters of the loan including the duration, size, and purpose of lending.

It may indeed be useful to view the rate of interest as merely one of the conditions relating to a credit transaction. The understanding of the personalistic relationship between lenders and borrowers is equally important because it has an impact on other markets also, besides its effect on the credit transaction. Credit interlinkage allows lending to affect prices in other markets and enables the lenders to engage in conjoint appropriation of returns from various economic activities. As a result, there is great diversity in credit arrangements and in the form that the returns from lending accrue to the lender.

In the final analysis, the debate regarding interest rates charged by informal lenders is far from settled. Despite the evidence presented by several empirical studies on the subject, it is quite difficult to make any comparative analyses since the sample databases and the methods of computation of interest charges differ on the basis of the particular analyst's construct. Moreover, the pervasive effect of market interlinkage on effective interest rates is most often overlooked entirely.

Notes

1. This is similar to the nature of South Kanara's *holi* loans in India where the loan is taken in rice at any time of the year and is repaid with interest in paddy after the harvest of when the loan was taken (Nagaraj 1985, Basu 1989).

2. Basu (1989) presented an alternative approach for interest rates and suggests the importance of loan duration. He argued that a borrower who takes a loan closer

to the repayment date (usually at harvest time) has a more inelastic demand for credit. The practice of giving holi loans in India is thus viewed as implicit price discrimination, whereby individuals with inelastic demand for credit can effectively borrow only for shorter loan periods and become subjected to a higher (implicit) interest charge.

3. Indeed, this "live mortgage" is the most complex of the credit arrangements since the loan period could extend indefinitely. If the probability of repayment is small due to the relative loan size, the loan transaction becomes a *de facto* sale of usufruct rights to the lender.

4. In certain cases, the interest rate is not explicitly stipulated although the terms of loan payment are set. For example, one sack of rice borrowed has to be paid back with three sacks of *palay* or unmilled rice. For our purposes, the in-kind goods are converted in nominal terms and the equivalent interest rate, r_c is calculated.

6

An Empirical Analysis of Sorting Behavior and of Rationing Rules

Market interlinkage among heterogeneous agents leads to specific sorting behavior of informal lenders in the credit circuit, as suggested in the theoretical model of Chapter 4. The empirical implications of borrower-sorting and quantity rationing are tested in this chapter.

Any market that rests on quantity rather than price closure involves rationing, and calls, therefore, for the existence of certain sorting rules. Price closure is ruled out in the credit market because of the adverse selection of risk that high, market-clearing interest rates may invite in transactions involving the promise to pay in the future. The different kinds of collateral as well as the great variety of interest rates observed both in formal and informal credit markets are not intended to fully eliminate the risk of default, but rather to make various categories of non-homogeneous borrowers observationally equivalent. The sorting rules are then applied to differentiate among the sets of observationally equivalent borrowers. Moreover, specific rationing rules are applied within each set of observationally equivalent borrowers in order to allocate each lender's loanable funds under conditions of excess demand.

The theoretical model presented in Chapter 4 led to a set of testable hypotheses relating to the profit-maximizing behavior of two types of non-homogeneous agents, trader-lenders and farmer-lenders. The predictions of the model are specifically tested by differentiating the borrowers from the point of view of wealth (rich and poor households) and the level of agricultural productivity of the area in which they operate (developed and marginal areas). There are good grounds for using a wealth criterion to differentiate among borrowers. The specific resource position of the borrower-household determines not only its default propensity but also preferences among other contractual covenants such as collateral that might be tendered. The borrower's economic status provides therefore relevant information on the position of the farmer in credit relationships.

General economic conditions also have a substantial impact on the credit terms since they define the institutional framework and thus affect the transaction costs of credit. The differentiation in the economic environment is likely to be reflected in behavioral differences among the agents in the credit circuit.

Since each of the 111 households in the Survey has contracted a number of loans, normally with more than one lender, we can rigorously test for the correspondence between different types of lenders and types of borrowers to investigate sorting patterns. Similarly, by making the size of the loan granted in each transaction a function of the household's observable characteristics, we can test for the rationing rules that apply in our sample.

Sorting Behavior

The profit maximization model specified the objective function of trader-lenders as joint maximization in their primary activity, merchandizing, and their secondary activity, moneylending. The objective function of the farmer-lenders, on the other hand, involves gaining control over the usufruct of land, along with maximizing profits from the secondary activity of moneylending. The divergence in the objective functions leads to predictable behavioral differences.

Trader-lenders are expected to behave so as to maximize their inventories of tradable output thus securing the largest possible share of the output trading market. This leads them to converting all of their operating capital, directly or indirectly, into output right after harvest. Such behavior implies not only interlinking credit with output but also sorting potential borrowers positively with respect to their marketable surplus and negatively with respect to their probability of default. Given the distinction of the borrowers into rich and poor, the expectation is that profit maximization of trader-lenders would lead to transacting with the former. Rich farmer-borrowers are more likely to have large marketable output that not only makes interlinkage possible, but also decreases the per-unit supervision costs of the trader-lender. They are more likely to be regular sellers of output, and the regularity with which rich farmers deal with traders often leads to historically developed personal ties. Among observationally equivalent borrowers, credit allocation by trader-lenders may be determined by the expected size of marketed surplus. The loan size is therefore an increasing function of the borrower's expected output. When it comes to interest rate charges, trader-lenders may or may not raise interest rates to compensate for risk, since the resulting increase in profits may be fully offset by the increase in the probability of default following adverse selection of risk.

Farmer-lenders, on the other hand, consider as attractive credit targets farmers who will default under certain circumstances and who are willing to bear the consequences of the default. Poor farmers have small marketable surplus to offer in a tied-in sale of output and are more likely to offer the usufruct of land in the transaction instead. They are more vulnerable to the fluctuation of the market or the weather and more likely to seek distress loans. Poor farmers are politically weak and less likely to increase the lender's contract enforcement costs of foreclosure if default becomes necessary. The expectation therefore is that profit maximization will lead farmer-lenders to dealing with poor borrowers. Nevertheless, given the complexities of the process of transferring land usufruct rights, credit rationing by farmer-lenders with regard to the size of the loan and the interest charges may or may not follow the predicted lending pattern of trader-lenders.

Conditional Probabilities Tests

The first set of tests of the sorting behavior of lenders is based on estimating conditional probabilities. The probability *P[.]* is said to be *conditional* if the occurrence of the event *A* is subject to the information that event *B* has occurred. Conditioning with the information that event *B* has occurred simply introduces a smaller probability space; thus the adjective "conditional" is used to refer to the reduced model. The frequency approach is used to estimate *P[.]*; that is, for a given N number of occurrences for which events *A* and *B* are defined, *P[A | B]* represents the proportion of occurrences in which *A* and *B* occurred jointly. In other words,

$$P[A \mid B] = \frac{N_{ab}}{N_b} \qquad (6.1)$$

where N_b denotes the number of occurrences of the event *B* in the *N* occurrences of the random experiment and N_{ab} denotes the number of occurrences of the event $A \cap B$ in the *N* occurrences.

Conditional probabilities regarding credit disbursements of farmer-lenders and trader-lenders are computed using our sample survey data. We want to know what is the probability, for example, that a farm household borrows from a trader-lender (event *A*), given that the household belongs to the poor income category (event *B*). Or alternatively, what is the probability that an informal lender provides a loan to a poor farmer (event *A*), given that the source of loan is a trader-lender (event *B*). A skewed pattern of conditional probabilities would suggest that credit allocation is not done randomly among different classes of borrowers.

The estimated conditional probabilities presented in Table 6.1 illustrate the pattern of borrowing by different household categories. In both marginal and developed areas, the probability that poor borrowers obtained their loans from farmer-lenders is higher than the probability of their having borrowed from any other source. The reverse is true for rich

TABLE 6.1   Estimated Probabilities of Household Receiving Loan from Lender Type by Income Class and Study Area

Income Class	Landlord	Farmer-Lender	Trader-Lender	Others*
Marginal area				
Poor	0.167	0.648	0.073	0.114
Middle	0.045	0.391	0.481	0.079
Rich	0.000	0.564	0.943	0.000
Developed area				
Poor	0.042	0.515	0.317	0.123
Middle	0.007	0.364	0.529	0.114
Rich	0.000	0.117	0.766	0.115

*These include local government officials, employees, businessmen, school-teachers, etc.

borrowers. The probability that they received their loans from farmer-lenders is relatively low while the probability that they borrowed from traders is fairly close to one. The position of middle-income borrowers is consistently between the two extremes. Moreover, controlling for the initial endowments of the borrower, whether rich or poor, the probability that the lender is a trader increases as one moves from marginal to developed areas. This pattern suggests that as a borrower moves up on the development transition matrix, whether by income or by productivity of land, a shift in borrowing occurs from farmer-lenders to trader-lenders.

TABLE 6.2   Estimated Probabilities of Lender Type Granting Loan to Household by Income Class and Study Area

Income Class	Farmer-Lender	Trader-Lender
Marginal area		
Poor	0.748	0.086
Middle	0.205	0.193
Rich	0.046	0.711
Developed area		
Poor	0.557	0.167
Middle	0.247	0.194
Rich	0.196	0.640

Table 6.2 presents the estimated probabilities regarding credit disbursements of farmer-lenders and trader-lenders. The results suggest that in general, farmer-lenders tend to allocate a greater volume of their loans to poor farmers and trader-lenders do so to rich farmers. This finding further confirms the existence of implicit sorting of borrowers by the lenders.

Comparing the probabilities under different agricultural environments we find the divergence in probability estimates slightly wider in marginal areas than in developed areas. This suggests that although a clear pattern of borrower sorting exists, there is more flexibility on the part of informal lenders with regard to borrower preference in the developed area than in the marginal area. In particular, farmer-lenders in the developed area seem to be more flexible with respect to borrower preference than their counterparts in the marginal area, lending to rich borrowers with greater probability than the latter. This *modified* sorting behavior may be explained by the effect that the economic environment has on the patterns of competition. The growth of trading activity that accompanies an increase in productivity leads to the development of intricate trading networks with diverse middleman activities. The active participation of farmer-lenders in the process of providing intermediation services to trader-lenders in the developed areas leads to personalistic relationships through financial layering. If farmer-lenders act as agents for trader-lenders, they are expected to partly, at least, adopt their objective function by sorting borrowers who are expected with high probability to deliver their output at harvest time. Such borrowers are more likely to be found in the developed area; and therefore the agency relationship is more common there.

Similarly, traders are more likely to lend to poor borrowers in the developed area than their counterparts in the marginal area for several reasons. One possible explanation for this modified sorting behavior is the rapid expansion of commodity production in the developed area. The increase in productivity resulting from the introduction of irrigation and the attendant adoption of modern technologies has brought about an overall increase in the volume of marketable output. This leads to faster growth of trade and to the entry of more traders, which intensifies competition. The presence of new traders in the area with little or no prior knowledge about the characteristics of farmer-borrowers in turn, could have led to further extension of credit at the margin, namely, to poor farmers.

Another explanation relates to the reduction in production risk resulting from the presence of agricultural infrastructure in the developed areas, such as irrigation. The decrease in the weather-related risk makes all farmers in developed areas, including the poor ones, more creditworthy borrowers.

Analysis of Variance Tests

The analysis of variance method (ANOVA) decomposes the variance of a characteristic of a population into the between-group variance and the within-group variance. The test for the equality of the between-group mean and the within-group mean is based on analyzing the significance of the variance around the respective means of population characteristics.

Presently the characteristics in question are total household income for the production period (Y), total land area under cultivation (N_c), total land area owned (N_o), and gross harvest (Q). This information exists for all households in the survey and for the wet cropping season 1983-84.

The source of each loan received by a farm household is identified by type of major lender, i.e., farmer-lender or trader-lender. By summing the total indebtedness of each household, a binary classification is formed, depending on whether less or more than 50 percent of the household's loans (by value) were received from farmer-lenders or from trader-lenders. Assuming a normal sample for each of the groups, ANOVA is used on the means of different characteristics of borrower households for group-wise comparisons for unbalanced or non-orthogonal design.[1] In other words, we analyze the variance to test for the equality of the respective means. This helps determine whether or not the economic status and resource position of the borrower-household, as proxied by the specific characteristics included, affects the decision of a particular lender to enter into credit exchange relations. The Duncan multiple-range test is also performed to determine whether the group-wise differences in means are significant at specified (5 percent in this case) levels of significance.

Table 6.3 presents the means of the household characteristics of interest and the results of the Duncan multiple-range tests indicating the significance of the group-wise differences in means. Looking at the variables size of cultivated land (N_c), and gross output (Q) first, we observe that households with higher means in these characteristics consistently get more than 50 percent of their credit from trade-lenders, while households with lower characteristic means get more than 50 percent of their loans from trader-lenders. Moreover, within the classification of households that borrow from trader-lenders, the difference in means is significant between the groups that get less/more than 50 percent of their loans from that source, whether for the N_c or the Q characteristic. Similarly the group differences in means for both characteristics are also significant for households classified by the proportion of their loans they receive from farmer-lenders. This is not surprising since farmer-lenders are willing to accept collateral other than the borrower's harvest.

The characteristic household income (Y) presents the same pattern: households with higher mean incomes receiving more than 50 percent of their credit from trader-lenders and, conversely, households with lower

TABLE 6.3 Results of Anova-Duncan Multiple Range Analysis Characteristics by Borrower and Lender Type

Borrower Characteristics	Borrower Category[a]	
	Received Less Than 50 Percent of Loans from Lender Type	Received More Than 50 Percent of Loans from Lender Type
Trader-lenders		
Income, Y (pesos)	6,043*	12,572*
Size of land cultivated, N_c (hectares)	1.28*	2.26*
Size of land owned, N_o (hectares)	0.66	0.76
Gross output, Q (kilograms)	4,516*	8,541*
Farmer-lenders		
Income, Y (pesos)	9,027	5,142
Size of land cultivated, N_c (hectares)	1.77*	1.13*
Size of land owned, N_o (hectares)	0.83	0.38
Gross output, Q (kilograms)	6,606*	4,072*

[a]The asterisk (*) indicates that the Duncan multiple-range test finds the group means to be significantly different at 5 percent level.

mean incomes receiving more than 50 percent of their loans from farmer-lenders. While the difference in mean incomes, however, is significant between the group borrowing less/more than 50 percent of their loan volume from trader-lenders, it is not significant, respectively, within the classification of households borrowing from farmer-lenders. This finding again confirms the conclusion reached in the previous section that farmer-lenders have a broader range of borrower preferences, presumably because they often act also as middlemen, performing services of financial layering for trader-lenders. Moreover, the farmer-lenders' definitional characteristics of creditworthy borrowers include not only repayment ability, but also willingness to tender a certain kind of collateral, land usufruct rights.

The characteristic of land ownership (N_o) also shows the predictable differences in means between households that borrow mostly from trader-lenders and those that borrow mostly from farmer-lenders, but the group means within a lender category do not vary significantly for the groups of less/more than 50 percent of their loan volume. The explanation probably lies in the fact that land ownership is not perfectly correlated with land under cultivation, and therefore is not a correlate of output or income either.

Rationing Rules

The statistical results just presented provide empirical support for the validity of the sorting proposition. They do not explain, however, how lenders ration credit within an observationally equivalent group of borrowers, given the excess demand that characterizes the credit market. Following the respective maximization hypotheses advanced for the two types of lenders, the test revolves around the relation between the size of the loan and borrower characteristics that proxy capacity to repay the loan, such as income and the agricultural environment in which he operates. More specifically, since trader-lenders are concerned with the ability of borrowers to service outstanding debts, they make the size of the loan an increasing function of the borrower's income. This is captured in a loglinear regression model in which the size of loans provided by trader-lenders is the dependent variable, W_{st}, and the borrower's income, Y_i, is the explanatory variable.[2] Regional differences in environmental and technical conditions are also taken into account by using a dummy variable, D_i. The regression equation is:

$$W_{st} = a + b_1 Y_i + d D_i + u ,\qquad\qquad (6.2)$$

with variables in logarithmic form.

The estimated coefficients are reported in Table 6.4. The coefficient of income is positive and significant, indicating the expected relationship between trader-lender's loan size and income level of the borrower. It implies that traders tend to offer larger loans to farmers with higher incomes. Since this is a logarithmic function, the regression coefficient, b_1, represents the loan elasticity with respect to income. The dummy variable is not significant, indicating that traders in the two areas do not differ significantly in their credit allocation patterns.

An implication of the transaction costs hypothesis is that effective interest rates are inversely related to the level of income and directly related to the probability of default. The relationship to income arises from the expectation that the richer the borrower, the lower is the cost of supervision and monitoring. Conversely, poorer borrowers not only have higher supervision costs, they also have a higher probability of default that should be reflected in higher interest rates. Beyond a certain point, however, the higher the interest rate, the more likely adverse selection of risk becomes, and then the causality between interest rates and incidence of default is reversed. These hypotheses are tested by formulating the logarithmic relations in (6.3) and (6.4) as:

$$r_m = a + b_2 \, Y_i + d \, D_i + u \tag{6.3}$$

$$r_m = a + c_1 \, k_i + d \, D_i + u \tag{6.4}$$

with r_m being the effective monthly rate of interest on the loan and k_i the *ex post* observed incidence of default. The variables are in logarithmic form except for r_m.

The results reported in Table 6.4 confirm both implications of the transaction costs hypothesis. The coefficient of income in the effective interest rate regression is negative and significant, while the default rate is positively related to the interest rate, at a high level of significance. The direction of causality, however, cannot be tested in the two-variable model of equation (6.4). The dummy variables are not significant in either equation.

In contrast to trader-lenders, farmer-lenders are willing and able to lend to poor borrowers. The potential gains consist not only of interest earnings, but more importantly, of the opportunity to gain access over borrowers' land. Since land transfer can take place only when the borrower has defaulted, farmer-lenders find it advantageous to discriminate in favor of borrowers that have a high default propensity. Table 6.5 shows that the recorded cases of land mortgage involve overwhelmingly poor households, especially so in the marginal areas where the majority of land mortgages were observed. Moreover, the estimated probability that a household mortgages a portion of its land is high for poor households, with probability in the marginal areas being twice that in developed areas. The susceptibility of poor farmers to land foreclosure makes them attractive to farmer-lenders.

TABLE 6.4 Results of Least-Squares Regression Analysis for Trader-Lender Loans, All Households[a]

Equation	Dependent Variable	Intercept	Y_i	k_i	D
1.	W_{st} (7.925)	2.425 (1.79)	0.410* (3.24)	—	-0.298 (-1.18)
	F = 5.64* (2,86 d.f.) Adj. R^2 = 0.15				
2.	r_m (14.651)	28.457* (3.83)	-2.181* (-2.90)	—	3.199 (1.53)
	F = 5.66* (2,86 d.f.) Adj. R^2=0.11				
3.	r_m (14.651)	6.932* (6.25)	—	1.169 (1.93)	1.62 (0.72)
	F = 3.37* (2,86 d.f.) Adj. R^2 = 0.09				

All variables are in natural log form except for r_m. Asterisked coefficients are significant at 95 percent level. Numbers in parentheses indicate the mean values for dependent variable, t-ratios for the explanatory variables, and the degrees of freedom for F.

Variables are defined as:

W_{st} = Size of loan provided by trader-lender in pesos.
r_m = Effective monthly rate of interest on the loan.
Y_i = Household income for the period in pesos.
k_i = The incidence of default.
D = Dummy variable taking the value 0 for developed areas and 1 for marginal areas.

[a]There are 97 trader-loans in total. However, due to missing values, only 89 observations are used.

TABLE 6.5 Estimated Probabilities of Households with Land Mortgages by Income Class and Study Area

	Marginal Area			Developed Area		
Income Class	Number	Percent	Probability of Belonging to Income Class	Number	Percent	Probability of Belonging to Income Class
Poor	15	94	.4411	5	56	.2052
Middle	1	6	.0909	3	33	.1579
Rich	—	—	.0000	1	11	.0625
Total	16	100		9	100	
Probability of belonging in the study area			.3265			.1451

Three regression models, corresponding to those of equations (6.2) to (6.4) are formulated to test the implications of the hypothesized farmer-lender behavior:

$$W_{sf} = a + b_3 Y_i + c_2 k_i + d D_i + u, \tag{6.5}$$

$$r_m = a + b_4 Y_i + d D_i + u, \text{ and} \tag{6.6}$$

$$r_m = a + c_3 k_i + d D_i + u, \tag{6.7}$$

where the variables are in logarithmic form; W_{sf} is the volume of loans household i receives from farmer-lenders; and the other variables are as defined previously.

The results reported in Table 6.6 confirm the implications of the hypothesis advanced above. The size-of-loan equation (6.5) is of interest because, contrary to the positive and strong relationship with income revealed in the case of trader-lenders, it shows a weak and negative relationship. The same equation shows a positive and significant relationship with the incidence of default. This confirms the discussion in the previous section associating incidence of default with accumulation of a sizable loan by poor borrowers. The loan size is likely to have a positive effect on default since the larger the loan relative to the borrower's income, the more susceptible the borrower becomes to default and, hence, the weaker is his resistance to the mortgage of land or transfer of his usufruct rights.

TABLE 6.6   Results of Least-Squares Regression Analysis for Farmer-Lender Loans, All Households[a]

Equation	Dependent Variable	Intercept	Y_i	k_i	D
4.	W_{sf} (6.833)	7.710* (3.66)	-0.27 (-1.22)	0.510* (2.51)	-0.89* (-2.54)
	F = 4.57* (3,95 d.f.) Adj. R^2 = 0.16				
5.	r_m (18.821)	-17.398* (-2.73)	4.247* (3.65)	—	1.39 (1.41)
	F = 6.71* (2,96 d.f.) Adj. R^2 = 0.14				
6.	r_m (18.821)	16.53* (7.29)	—	-4.699* (-6.18)	3.033 (1.82)
	F = 7.11* (2,96 d.f.) Adj. R^2 = 0.16				

All variables are in natural log form except for r_m. Asterisked coefficients are significant at 95 percent level. Numbers in parentheses indicate the mean values for the dependent variable, t-ratios for the explanatory variables, and the degrees of freedom for F.

Variables are defined as:

W_{sf} = Size of loan provided by farmer-lender in pesos.
r_m = Effective monthly rate of interest on the loan.
Y_i = Household income for the period in pesos.
k_i = The incidence of default.
D = Dummy variable taking the value 0 for developed areas and 1 for marginal areas.

[a]There are 107 farmer-lender loans. However, due to missing values, only 99 observations are used respectively. Mortgage loans included with zero effective interest rate.

Again contrary to the behavior of trader-lenders, the estimated relationship of equation (6.6) between effective interest rate and the level of income is positive. This again confirms the earlier discussion on interest-rate concessions that farmer-lenders are willing to make to poor households in order to advance a loan that eventually might lead to default. As indicated by the estimated coefficients of equation (6.7), the default rate tends to be higher at lower interest rate levels — presumably because farmer-lenders tend to charge low interest rates to borrowers with low incomes. The findings of both equations document a strategy adopted by farmer-lenders that aims at weakening the borrower's resistance to land mortgage. A borrower who wants to avoid land transfer is inclined to spread loan demand over several lenders and thus reduce individual loan amounts. This can be countered by the farmer-lender adopting a preemptive strategy of offering lower interest rates, allowing rollover of defaulted loans, or simply offering lenient terms of credit.

The economic implications of these findings are significant in that they describe the distinct behavior of trader-lenders and farmer-lenders on borrower sorting and on quantity rationing. The behavior of the latter in specific would have otherwise been described as counter-intuitive or irrational. Within the framework of the new institutional economics and the transaction costs hypothesis, however, it turns out to be unexceptionably transitive behavior. The fact that farmer-lenders offer larger loans at relatively low interest rates to the lower-income farmers certainly contradicts the conventional theory of interest rate determination, which states that the unusually high interest rates on informal loans may be explained largely by high risk premia. If this were true, one would have expected that the poorer the borrower, or the higher his propensity to default, the higher the interest rate charged (as is the case with trader-lenders). But then the conventional theory is predicated on the assumption that interest charges fully reflect the returns to lending.

The preceding discussion serves to highlight the importance of distinguishing between different types of lenders and borrowers. One of the key points to emerge from this study is that lenders do not have the same economic considerations; nor do they treat all borrowers uniformly. They also do not have the same criterion of what is a "creditworthy" borrower. Variations in interest charges therefore cannot be explained by identifying risk differences among borrowers alone. Understanding the specific characteristics of lenders, and how their economic positions determine attitudes toward risk and lending behavior, is a crucial prerequisite of any attempt to understand the great diversity that exists in credit relations.

Notes

1. "Unbalanced design" means that the cells of the two-way classification do not have the same number of observations.

2. The assumption is that the borrower's income earned during the period, Y_p serves as a proxy to his permanent income, which is the theoretically appropriate variable. Moreover, the implication is that the survey information on income is the same with the information on the borrower's income that the lender possesses.

7

Conclusions and Policy Implications

Asymmetries in the allocation of credit are all-pervasive, both in developed and in developing countries. Such asymmetries as are documented for the Philippines are especially pronounced. The allocation of credit by the formal sector, for example, distinctly favors non-agriculture: agriculture, with an average share in GDP of 30 percent in the period 1966-1984, accounted only for 8 percent of the share of formal credit. Within non-agriculture, the commercial and industrial activities, especially those undertaken by the larger firms, receive the lion's share of credit. Within agriculture, the size-preference of lenders is again visible, while the sectoral allocation of credit favors export and commercial crops.

Such asymmetries, and others highlighted in Chapter 3, have been interpreted in the past as symptoms of "urban bias" or as evidence of "financial repression" and have been associated with overt government acts of commission or omission. Regulation of financial intermediaries, government intervention in the credit market, and mandatory ceilings in the rate of interest are usually held responsible for financial repression. The prescribed remedy is financial liberalization, deregulation, and the removal of government intervention, especially from the area of setting interest rates on deposits and loans. Freeing interest rates to restore equilibrium in the supply and demand for credit is especially important since low, or even worse, negative interest rates lead to political patronage, monopolization of credit, and repressive effects on technology adoption.

Many of the issues raised by the financial repression approach are valid. Still, its exclusive preoccupation with government myopia instead of a broader interest in institutional structure often leads to the wrong type of policy recommendations. Attributing, for example, the fragmented capital markets not to inherent characteristics of the credit transaction but to repressive government policies, leads to transposing the simplistic "set the prices right" argument from co-temporal transactions to inter-temporal transactions that involve a promise to repay in the future. Such a transposition is not always legitimate.

This book has viewed credit within the new institutional economics framework in which transactions involving an extraordinary component of trust, the credibility of the promise to repay in the future, entail also a significant component of trust-specific transaction costs. The structural distortions observed in credit markets are results of institutional responses to overcome inherent incentive problems. While in developed countries, market infrastructure and social and economic institutions allow for establishment of trust, in developing countries there is a huge infrastructural and institutional vacuum. The production mode of the formal sector is thus predicated on the existence of well-developed market institutions, while the informal sector deals in the formal infrastructural vacuum that remains.

It is in this sense that the "price-quality" theorem of Stiglitz and Weiss (1981) becomes applicable. And thus arises the need for government regulation of credit markets and the requirement that creditors charge a non-equilibrium interest rate — implying the existence of excess demand and necessity for quantity rationing. Moreover, the new institutional economics approach to credit attributes the constraints to the expansion of the formal sector to inherent characteristics of the prevailing macroeconomic environment in general and of credit markets in particular that increase transactions costs and make the credit contract a personalistic relationship. Correspondingly, the residuality approach to the role of the informal sector implies that informal credit comes into action to fill the gap that the formal financial sector has left. The informal market is conceded the vast loan demand of borrowers who do not satisfy the "bankability of risk" requirements of the formal sector. This residuality approach is illustrated in cases where the informal sector expands into areas where the formal sector traditionally does not venture, such as smallholder credit extended by trader-lenders or by farmer-lenders. It is also illustrated in cases where the formal sector abruptly withdraws, leaving a credit vacuum to be filled by the informal sector. As an example, shrinking the coverage of Masagana-99 loans from 800,000 to only 108,000 households in a period of a few years in the late 1970s led to the expansion of the informal sector to fill the gap by providing three-quarters of the total agricultural credit, as compared to the one-third it was providing before.

Implications of the New Institutional Economics Approach

According to the new institutional economics approach, the operation of effective credit markets is based on a foundation of trust. The government plays an important role in creating trust, which is part of the social infrastructure and to varying degrees enters the operation of all markets.

More specifically, in credit markets, the role of government as an umpire and lender of last resort becomes important. Auditing and monitoring rules, credible deposit guarantees, and regulations that intend to keep the assets of the banking system fairly liquid, all tend to increase public trust, attract deposits, and enable loans. So does increased accessibility to the bank, such as a convenient location, long working hours, and hassle-free withdrawals on demand. The same purpose is served by the trappings of prestige, from architecture to personal style. The problem that mobile credit officers have in mobilizing deposits, as opposed to making loans, is not only the Zambian reaction of "the truck took our savings and went away"; it is also the Pakistani attitude that "deposits require an iron door and a marble counter-top."

The real issue arising in financial markets is not regulation or non-regulation, but rather what is the appropriate and the optimum degree of regulation. In fact, studies of financial liberalization policies in Chile, Argentina, and Uruguay demonstrate that financial reforms, if not properly designed, cause further instability of the financial system thus magnifying the underlying macroeconomic instability (Blejer and Gil-Diaz 1986, Calvo 1986, Yotopoulos 1988, Fry 1988, Cho and Khatkhate 1989). Liberalization of interest rates is always the first target of banking deregulation schemes. Could it be that this emphasis, after all, is entirely appropriate? If, as the price-quality theorem states, there is an optimal, as opposed to a maximum, interest rate that lenders charge, would not one expect banks to exercise prudence and self-policing in setting their rates?

The risk in interest rates does not come so much from the lending side, as it comes from the borrowing operations of formal financial institutions. Liberalization of deposit rates sets off a competitive drive by banks for borrowing. Banks that have access only to relatively expensive money (along with those that are relatively inefficient in their operations) have an incentive to charge the higher (than optimum) lending rates in order to break even. In the process they adversely select risks in their lending portfolio, and become prone to default. The impact of unanticipated adverse selection of risk among borrowers and moral hazard among lenders reflects the inherent limitations of financial liberalization. This is not the problem only of the U.S. Savings and Loan Associations in the mid-1980s. It has been an especially serious problem in the Philippines where banking deregulation has been enthusiastically promoted and has been actively practiced since 1981.

Deregulation in the Philippines so far has taken on the form of lifting of interest rate restrictions, setting of the rediscount rate at market levels, and limiting credit subsidies and credit quotas. Such reforms were inspired from the widespread belief that financially repressive regimes are inefficient and ineffective because government interventions are generally circumvented by financial institutions through various devices. While this may be true, the importance of a stable macroeconomic environment and of price stability as necessary preconditions for the success of financial liberalization policies cannot be underestimated. Similarly, the development of institutional infrastructure that promotes trust cannot be overlooked. Provisions for facilitating the flow of information, liberalization of property rights through agrarian reform, an effective legal enforcement system, and an appropriate regulatory mechanism to carefully monitor and evaluate financial behavior are prerequisites of financial liberalization; they are not superceded by it.

The high real interest rates in the Philippines were induced at least partly by the severe monetary contraction following the liquidity crisis of the early 1980s. They were also abated by a sudden dose of liberalization which led to "overshooting" of both nominal and real interest rates, unwarranted by the fundamentals (Cho and Katkhate 1989: xvii), and which gave banks the opportunity to widen their real spreads (Lamberte 1987). High real interest rates can be as disequilibrating as highly repressed negative interest rates.

In the short term, the market orientation of interest rates has adversely affected the current operations and status of those banks that were traditionally dependent on Central Bank funds, and it has probably adversely affected the mix of risks in all bank portfolia. The increase in the rediscount rate has compounded the effect of the heavy and growing burdens of delinquent loans and arrearages. Bank failures have become endemic, with the number of operating banks declining from 1214 to 1055 between 1981 and 1985 (Tolentino 1986: 19). The rural banks have been the hardest hit. In fact, of the 890 operating rural banks in June 1986, 80 percent were adjudged by the Central Bank ineligible to approach the rediscount window because of problems relating to their capital structure. In the meantime, financial liberalization did not end the bias of commercial banks in favor of urban lending, thus intensifying the formal financial contraction in the rural sector.

Besides interest rate decontrol, proponents of financial liberalization favor removing restrictions of entry into the field, removing loan-targeting restrictions and broadening the type of operations a bank can engage in. One can advance persuasive free-competition arguments in favor of such policies. On the other hand, the underlying premise of the price-quality theorem and of the new institutional economics is that excessive competition in credit markets can lead to adverse selection of risk and to bank failures, with externalities that extend beyond the banks' immediate shareholders and depositors. The line between monopolistic exploitation and competitive default is thin and cannot be drawn with ideological and simplistic prescriptions about "setting the prices right."

The debate on the development and reform of the financial sector in developing countries is far from settled. The initial enthusiasm by the proponents of financial liberalization in the 1970s and 1980s is somewhat dampened by the growing skepticism among academics and disillusionment among policy advisers on the effectiveness of such reforms. The experience of the Philippines, among other developing countries, has been catalytic in this emerging change in ideology. And while it is widely acknowledged in the policy circles that the financial crisis in developing countries, such as the Philippines, emanated from wrong and inconsistent macro policies, the obverse question, whether financial reforms worsened the disequilibrium of the financial sector and exacerbated the crisis, is hardly ever asked.

Although the focus of financial reforms is the formal sector their impact extends to the informal sector as well and covers the financial system as a whole. Still the informal sector has not been specifically studied within the financial liberalization environment. The push for liberalization is said to be encouraged by the perceived efficiency and dynamism of the informal sector, attributed to a large extent to the lack of government regulation. The versatility of informal financial intermediation is supposed to be replicated for the formal sector through "universal banking," whereby commercial banks can diversify into investment banking, insurance, trading, and other sundry and sultry activities. Taking a lead from the informal sector, banks in the Philippines have attempted to interlink credit with other agricultural markets. The empirical analysis of informal credit leads to specific policy implications relating to such proposals.

Implications of the Analysis of Informal Credit Markets

The residuality approach of the informal sector advanced and tested for in this work has clear policy implications that are opposite to those derived from the marginality approach. The informal credit sector performs a useful economic function of filling in the credit needs that rationing in the formal sector has left unfulfilled. Our study demonstrates that the informal financial intermediation sector is extremely flexible and successfully adjusts to the prevailing economic conditions. Its contractual arrangements evolve by a particular selection of modes of economic behavior that are responsive to the imperfections of the market. It builds on existing personalistic relationships so that the essential requisite of credit contracts, namely trust, is more readily established. Trust is further enhanced by means of interlinked market arrangements and credit layering which allow for more credible enforcement of the contract. The informal sector is complementary, rather than competitive, to the formal sector. As a result it merits encouragement and support, as opposed to prohibition and prosecution.

Although there is great diversity and heterogeneity among rural economic agents in the informal credit markets, our study has shown the dominance of particular types of commercial lenders, namely the trader-lenders and farmer-lenders. The following discussion is thus based on the study of the behavior of these informal lenders.

The major advantage of informal lenders is that they can build a per-sonalistic relationship with their borrowers which enables them to hurdle the information barrier and the moral hazard problem, thus ensuring an extremely low loan default rate. The main disadvantage is that they rely on limited own or borrowed funds for their lending operations. The obvious solution is to release the constraint of informal-sector lenders by using them as conduits of formal-sector funds. This increases the layering of agricul-tural credit, a strong characteristic of the empirical cases we examined in previous chapters. In fact, there currently exist three official schemes in the Philippines that propose to use the informal sector as a conduit of credit extended by the formal sector.

The Quedan Guarantee Fund Board (QGFB) (formerly the Grains Quedan Special Financing Program) is an agency attached to the Ministry of Agri-culture and Food (MAF) that utilizes the *quedan,* or warehouse receipt, as a loan guarantee. Traders and millers who borrow from the banking system qualify for the guarantee of 80 percent of the loan value on the basis of grain stocks they hold in a bonded warehouse. The traders and millers in turn extend production loans to farmers, subject to the tie-in provision that (a portion of) the grain harvest be sold to a specified *quedan* operator. Pres-ently, the coverage of QGFB is extended to grains merchants and to farmers who are engaged in small-scale trading of output. By providing access to government funds, the QGFB augments the capital base of trader-lenders and farmer-lenders who, unlike the large and well-established palay traders, have little collateral to offer. Although the QGFB receives no government subsidies, it has been able to expand its operations and to leverage its relatively small capital base of 150 million pesos into covering loans totalling four times that amount. This is largely due to the 99 percent loan repayment record it has achieved, as shown in Table 7.1.

Two more low-cost special financing schemes are targeted mainly to agricultural input suppliers who are used as conduits for lending to farmers with loan interlinkage provisions. The Planters' Product Credit scheme (PPC) makes available to input suppliers a special credit line at 12 percent annual interest rate on the condition that they organize distribution chan-nels for fertilizer and pesticide credit to farmers. The credit extended by the dealer is tied to the purchase of the modern inputs of production with the purpose of encouraging the adoption of high-yielding technologies.

A similar scheme targets input suppliers, as well as traders, millers, and processors of agricultural commodities, and provides credit at greater government subsidy than the PPC scheme. The End Users'/Input Suppli-

TABLE 7.1 Summary Performance of Selected Credit Programs, Cumulative Data, as of September 1986 (million pesos)

Credit program	Total Loans Released	Total Loans Collected	Repayment Rate[a] (percent)
Quedan Financing for			
Traders/processors	1,767.3	1,625.5	99.8
Small farmers	6.1	3.6	92.6
Subtotal	1,773.4	1,629.1	
End Users/Input Suppliers Scheme under			
Intensified Rice Production Program[b]	46.8	32.2	89.0
Expanded Corn Program[c]	78.3	57.1	94.0
National Rootcrops Program[d]	6.6	1.5	—
Subtotal	131.7	90.8	

[a]Repayment rate is computed as percentage of loans repaid to loans matured x 100.
[b]Cumulative from Phases 1-4.
[c]Cumulative from Phases 84B to 86B.
[d]Cumulative from Phases 1 (1985) to 2 (1986).

Source: Emmanuel Esguerra, "On the Use of Informal Lenders as Conduits for Formal Credit: The Case of the National Agricultural Productivity Programs in the Philippines," Economics and Sociology Occasional Paper No. 1351, (Columbus: Ohio State University, May 1987), Table 3.

ers' Assistance scheme has been launched by the National Agricultural Productivity Program (NAPP) to provide credit to the conduits mentioned above (end users) at a rate of 6 percent per annum under the condition that they, in turn, extend production loans to farmers at a 15 percent per annum interest rate, inclusive of service charges of the agent bank. The loans of the intermediaries are normally tied to another market, depending on their relationship with the farmer-borrower. Agricultural processors, for example, may advance loans tied to the delivery of a specified quantity of output at harvest at a purchase price not lower than the government support price; input suppliers may tie the loans to the purchase of fertilizers or chemicals. The special relationship between the conduit and the borrower, the interlinkage of the loan, plus the fact that the intermediary is responsible for a 42 percent surcharge on defaulted loans, probably all account for the 92 percent recovery rate of the loans extended under this scheme (Table 7.1). The above schemes were implemented on the assumption that credit provision vis a vis the informal lenders will not only stimulate productivity growth and agricultural development, but also increase the flow of credit funds and provision of financial services to small farmers.

Implications of Market Interlinkage and Sorting

Our empirical analysis accounts for the extreme heterogeneity observed in credit contracts by distinguishing a number of agents and a variety of principal-agent relationships in our sample. The four main types of agents encountered — trader-lenders, farmer-lenders, rich borrowers, poor borrowers — are further distinguished depending on whether they operate in developed areas or in marginal areas, and whether they engage in unlinked credit, or they enter a contractual relationship that ties credit to another market, such as that for output, land, and inputs.

The theoretical analysis and empirical verification have confirmed the Stiglitz-Weiss theorem that the optimal rate of interest is below the market-clearing rate if the lender is interested in forestalling adverse selection of risk and default. A great variety of effective rates of interest are calculated as applying to various kinds of principal-agent relationships. A consistent pattern however emerges: interest rates are lower for linked than for unlinked loans, and they are higher at marginal than at developed areas. The behavior of trader-lenders is distinctly different from that of farmer-lenders, since the former try to avoid adverse selection of risk, while the latter invite it under certain conditions. As a result, in trader-lender interlinkage with output, the interest rate is a decreasing function of income and an increasing function of the probability of default. In farmer-lender credit, which is interlinked with land, the effective interest rate is an increasing function of income, except at low levels of initial indebtedness where low interest rates are used as an "attracting nuisance" in order to facilitate debt accumulation that triggers in the collateral.

Quantity closure is a characteristic of all credit markets; it implies capital rationing. The identification of non-homogeneous agent groups in our study enables us to investigate the rationing rules. In both marginal and developed areas the probability that poor farmers obtained their loans from farmer-lenders is greater than that for rich farmers. Trader-lenders, on the other hand, tend to allocate a greater proportion of their loans to rich farmers. More generally, as borrowers move up the development transition matrix, whether by income or by productivity of land, a shift in borrowing occurs from farmer-lenders to trader-lenders. This constitutes a consistent pattern, whether the correlate of mean income, mean output, or mean size of cultivated land is applied to various classes of borrowers. Quantity rationing implies that wider credit accessibility may not necessarily take place under the informal lenders' conduit schemes. Any additional funds available to the informal lender may only result in bigger loans to the same number of farmers.

Credit layering is another corollary of the personalistic relationship of informal intermediaries. The loans of trader-lenders (whether input dealers, ricemillers, or wholesalers) extended to their farmer *sukis* and linked to intermediation services represent informal financial layering and create a sub-category of farmer-lenders, the marketing-agent lenders, or *mga piyudor*. These lenders assume dual role as farmer-lenders on their own account and as intermediaries for a trader who entrusts them with substantial amounts of capital to relend. In this dual role, they may link a loan to the transfer of land rights, acting on their own account; and/or they can accept loan repayment in kind at the time of harvest, acting as the traders' agents. Credit-layering means that capital passes through several hands before finally reaching the small farmer-borrowers. A legitimate question that needs to be answered in this regard is what proportion of the credit subsidy under the End Users'/Input Suppliers' Assistance scheme, for example, is captured by the trader-recipient and the marketing agent-lenders? Moreover, does the likelihood of diverting credit to unauthorized uses increase as the intermediation chain is lengthened?

In conclusion, interest rates, risk, probability of default and type of collateral, which all enter the formal-sector credit contract, are not sufficient to fully characterize the credit relationship. The investigation of informal credit, which evolves into a variety of principal-agent contracts, gives a fuller flavor of the credit relationship, including the specification of the rationing rules used by various agents as well as the practice of credit layering.

On How to Default or Not: Policy Implications

One can make a persuasive case that, individual maximization considerations aside, the broad availability of agricultural credit on terms that are affordable by small farmers and do not lead to default has a positive value for social welfare. There are various channels through which lack of agricultural credit at the micro-level can have an impact on aggregate agricultural output. Lack of credit to a specific enterprise can forestall an increase in agricultural productivity by limiting access to modern inputs. Credit restrictions can lower productivity by forcing the sale of farm equipment, reducing maintenance expenditure, leading to sub-optimal use of inputs, or forcing a shift to sub-optimal crop mixes in order to reduce operating expenses. Since land can be cultivated at any one time by one operator, lack of credit for individual operators can conceivably be aggregated to a net loss in output. This implies that individual agricultural projects that can attract financing are imperfect substitutes for one another.

The micro-economic effects described above could be reversed when lack of credit leads to default and the land is transferred to another operator who has better access to credit. This usually implies land consolidation and an increase in average farm-size. In developing countries, however, foreclosure of small farms that are beyond a minimum size may have some negative externalities as well as negative equity consequences. The often-encountered negative relationship between farm size and productivity may conceal a number of other factors (from superior technical efficiency to better quality of land and easier access to reservoirs of cheap family labor) that may favor small-size farms. If maximizing output per unit of land is the social maximand — as opposed to the usual cost-minimization for an appropriately specified and evaluated set of inputs — public policy may not be neutral in the question of default or no default. In addition, increasing land concentration in economies with existing wide income disparities only exacerbates political instability.

The empirical investigation of interlinked credit in this case has a crucial policy implication. Interlinkage, like any other principal-agent relationship, has the characteristic that the lender can by his actions affect the outcome of the contract. With the outcome in question being the probability of default, the farmer-lender interlinkage of credit with land becomes an appropriate object for public scrutiny. Ironically, the risk with farmer-lenders lies in charging low interest rates initially and making other concessions to farmers for the purpose of increasing the total size of their indebtedness to the value of the land collateral; once this point is reached, they have an incentive to charge high interest rates in order to assist default and foreclosure on the collateral. This does not appear to be an unusual pattern in our sample survey. On the other hand, trader-lenders, given their maximization behavior, are likely to self-police against contractual stipulations that may lead to adverse selection of risk and default. This, however, does not mean that interest rates and other hidden charges they impose, such as the underpricing of farmers' output by traders and the overpricing of inputs by suppliers, are not a substantial drain on farmers' earnings. In this regard, the informal lenders' conduit schemes must be carefully re-examined for efficiency and equity as instruments of channeling credit.

Undoubtedly, financial markets, given their vital role in providing financial services to the population, require both government regulation and government assistance for improving their performance. But any rehabilitation policy package, whether it involves the formal institutions alone or includes the informal sector as well, must take into account the crucial impact that the current state of the economic environment has, especially on financial markets that are fragmented by nature. The existence of nurturing institutional and economic infrastructure is vital for financial intermediation in general. Lending to small farmers in particular becomes extremely risky and costly under conditions that are only too familiar in underdevelopment and poverty: absence of transport links and of support infrastructures like irrigation in many rural areas, unfavorable terms of trade for the agricultural sector, and uneven access to land and modern agricultural inputs. Remedying these deficiencies improves the overall economic viability of small borrowers which in the final analysis determines the reach of the formal and the effectiveness of both formal and informal financial intermediation.

Appendix: The Survey

Various aspects of informal credit markets have been empirically investigated in the literature. For the Philippines, for instance, a large body of informal credit data has been collected from extensive household surveys conducted by the Presidential Committee on Agricultural Credit (PCAC). Many of the empirical studies using this body of statistics have provided direct evidence of the complementary features of the informal sector as well as a general analysis of the informal credit market (TBAC 1981a, 1985, Quinones 1982). Other village surveys and microstudies that form part of anthropological and sociological research of small groups provide indirect evidence on the informal sector (Davis 1968, Szanton 1972, Keyes 1982, Russell 1985).

The implications of the new institutional economics approach about informal credit are rich and not easily amenable to direct tests with the data readily available. We specifically designed a survey (hereafter referred to as Survey) for the purpose of obtaining a broader array of data in order to test various implications of the new institutional economics hypotheses. The data derived from the Survey reflect the different economic positions of market agents in the production and distribution processes and cover the multiple dimensions of credit transactions. A description of the Survey method follows as well as the process of data categorization.

The Survey Method

The Survey was conducted in the first half of 1984. It involved two sources of information on the informal lenders' behavior—interviews with 111 farmer-borrowers (indirect), and interviews with the lenders (direct). The indirect source were the borrower-households in the sample who identified their credit source as trader-lenders, farmer-lenders, or other. This method of information gathering requires classification of all loans according to lender type as well as an examination of the credit terms. The direct source involved eight farmer-lenders and eight trader-lenders. Interviews with the farmer-lenders revealed that they perform the dual role of borrowers (from traders and landlords) and lenders in the credit circuit. Informal discussions conducted with trader-lenders touched upon their marketing activities as well.

The Survey respondents were drawn from fourteen villages (*barrios*) in five Philippine municipalities: Talavera and Jaen in the province of Nueva Ecija, Tigbauan and Oton in Iloilo, and Solana in Cagayan (see Map). The selection of the survey sites was made on the basis of two sampling criteria. First, the three provinces are primarily rice- and corn-producing regions. The fact that rice and corn cultivation is the main source of livelihood for a majority of Filipino farmers justified this selection. Of the total land area devoted to crop production, estimated at 13 million hectares in 1983, rice and corn production constitutes 6.3 million hectares or nearly one-half of the total (NEDA 1984). Secondly, the five municipalities were chosen to reflect the uneven pace of agricultural development and commercialization in the Philippines.

Data Collection Procedure

The system we designed to conduct the Survey involved five phases:

1) Review of existing baseline surveys of potential study sites prior to 1984 by the Ministry of Agrarian Reform and the International Rice Research Institute.

2) Pre-survey visit to the three provinces and informal interviews of randomly selected farm households as well as discussions with local village leaders in the potential study sites.

3) Assessment of field observation notes and design of a comprehensive farm household questionnaire with indirect questions pertaining to informal credit practices.

4) Data gathering and survey interviews at the study sites between February and June 1984 by means of a multi-visit household survey and participant observation.

5) Return to the study sites after a few weeks to conduct interviews with traders, rich farmers, landowners, and rural bank officials. Visits to the regional government agencies for collection of secondary data.

The objectives of the first three phases were familiarization with the five municipalities chosen and assessment of the importance of informal credit in farm household accounts. The highly sensitive nature of the topic required a systematic and indirect approach to gathering information about credit. Based on the field notes gathered in the second phase of the data collection process, a comprehensive questionnaire was developed to cover various aspects of household activities as well as case histories of their landholdings. We also delved into the social and economic relations in which the household is involved (for example, with landlords, merchants, and other farmers in the areas). This gave us insight into the mechanism of trust-building and the level of personalistic ties.

The household-borrower questionnaire was administered to both household head and their spouse, and consisted of questions on demo-

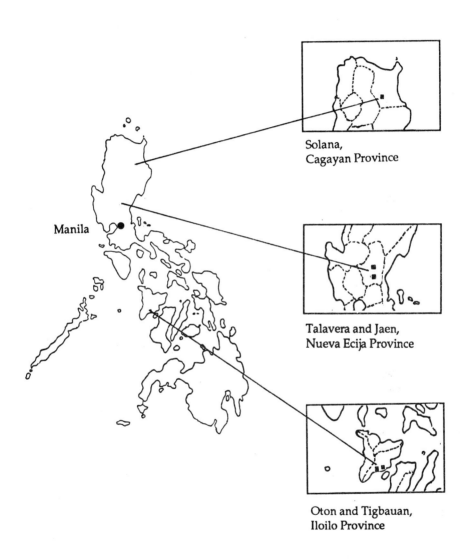

Solana,
Cagayan Province

Manila

Talavera and Jaen,
Nueva Ecija Province

Oton and Tigbauan,
Iloilo Province

Map of the Philippines and Study Areas

graphic information, consumption and production patterns, tenure status, and marketing practices. Questions regarding credit were included in all sections of the questionnaire. Because of its length, the Survey required about three to five sessions per respondent. In some cases, the questions were repeated in different formats to allow to double-check and thereby enhance the quality of the data. Most important, the multi-visit survey method afforded the interviewers more opportunity to get to know the farmers and gain their confidence over time. Field assistants from the village facilitated the familiarization process and also helped in the translation of the local dialect.

During the last phase, a separate visit was made to the areas, this time to conduct interviews with both formal and informal lenders. Although a structured questionnaire was devised, discussions were informal, just as with the farm households. Reluctance of informal lenders to provide accurate information about their working capital, assets, sources and disposal of funds, and in particular loan availability, made it difficult to tally the results in the same manner as that of the farm household survey. The questionnaire nonetheless served as a guideline for drawing out information about economic activities and involvement in moneylending. Insights into maximization behavior as well as general information about credit collection, number of borrowers, and default contingencies proved to be invaluable.

Secondary data, including monthly output and input prices, amortization payments, listing of land reform beneficiaries, and land classification were also collected and compiled from sources like Bureau of Agricultural Economics (BAEcon), and Ministry of Agrarian Reform (MAR) regional offices, National Food Authority (NFA), and National Economic and Development Authority (NEDA) regional branches, and the Bureau of Lands. This macro-economic information placed the village-level studies in the context of the overall regional situation and development plans.

Study Area Classification

The coexistence of developed regions, such as Nueva Ecija and irrigated portions of Iloilo with marginal regions, such as Cagayan, is characteristic of an agrarian economy with uneven development. While quantitative and qualitative changes have occurred in both production and exchange processes in the three provinces, the process of transformation has not been uniform. Uneven development has led to disparity in production conditions and agricultural productivity performance as well as to the coexistence of different production relations.

Yield risk, for instance, is relatively low in some parts of Nueva Ecija and Iloilo due to presence of gravity irrigation systems. Favorable agroclimatic conditions as well as a heavy infusion of modern inputs in the villages have led to increased productivity. Output production and market integration is stimulated not only by the introduction of new technology but also by the presence of agricultural extension programs and development of transport links. These changes in the production process have therefore prompted intensification of trading activity. The heightened pace of capital accumulation and the development of marketing channels in these developed areas have also brought about the need for spatial decentralization. These are stylized features over most of the developed areas in our study.

There are some parts of Nueva Ecija and Iloilo, the rainfed lowland and upland areas, that are more prone to the vagaries of nature, just like the villages in Solana, Cagayan. Most of these villages are located in the municipalities of Talavera in Nueva Ecija and Tigbauan in Iloilo. Water supply in these parts of all three provinces is almost wholly dependent on rainfall. Land use and output yield are affected by climatic conditions. Farmers in these regions use alternative cropping patterns that include upland crops like corn to accommodate landscape and rainfall variations. Traditional cultivation methods persist, and reliance on water buffaloes for land tillage is common. Crop care after planting is often minimal, and so is the application of fertilizer and pesticides. The distance of most farms from market centers and the lack of all-weather roads in these marginal areas pose serious difficulties in the marketing of farm products. These are stylized facts about the marginal areas in our study.

The uneven character of the study areas compels us to consider any variation in the patterns of credit that might reflect differences in production conditions and level of commercialization. For this reason, we classify the households in our survey into two study areas: 1) the *developed area*, which refers to high-productivity and more commercialized villages, and 2) the *marginal area*, which refers to the low-productivity and less commercialized villages. Table A.1 illustrates how the villages in the different municipalities are categorized into marginal and developed areas. The households in these villages are then grouped on the basis of the above criteria.

Forty-five percent of the total sample, or 49 farm households, belong to the *marginal* category. They are situated in villages characterized by poor transport links and by a lack of irrigation facilities as well as other support services. Although the average farm size is relatively large, these households have low yields.

Fifty-five percent, or a total of 62 farm households, belong to the *developed* area category. They are more integrated into the market, not only because of their proximity to the town centers, but also due to the massive infusion of new technology and accompanying support services during the last two decades. Intensive cultivation methods and the presence of irrigation have resulted in higher yields in spite of smaller farm size.

TABLE A.1 Study Area Classification of 111 Farm Households by Type of Production Method and Proximity to Town Markets, Selected Provinces

	Province Location of Households						
Characteristics	Cagayan (HH = 20)			Iloilo (HH = 38)		Nueva Ecija (HH = 53)	
Farm Location[a]	Upland Rainfed	Lowland Rainfed	Lowland Irrigated[b]	Plateau/ Upland Rainfed	Lowland Irrigated	Lowland Rainfed	Lowland Irrigated
Average farm size[c]	4.8	3.4	7.1	3.9	2.6	2.4	1.7
Usage of fertilizer[d]	low	low	medium/low	low	high	medium	high
Usage of tractor, thresher, etc.	none	none	partial	none	full	partial	full
Average rice field[e]	814	1176	3132	2764	4620	3552	4340
Access to nearest town market[f]	10-15	5-8	4-7	8-14	0.5-3	5-8	2-4
Number of households[g]	8	8	4	16	22	13	40
Study area classification	marginal	marginal	marginal	marginal	developed	marginal	developed

[a]Some households have landholdings situated in both upland and lowland areas. For purposes of categorization, households with more than 50 percent of land area in a particular location are considered.

[b]Irrigation is by means of water pumps.

[c]In hectares.

[d]Low usage is below 50 kgs of fertilizer per ha. Medium usage is 100-150 kgs of fertilizer per ha. High usage is more than 150 kgs of fertilizer per ha. Recommended level by the government is 250 kgs per ha.

[e](Unmilled) rice yield in kgs. per hectare.

[f]In kilometers.

[g]Total number of households in marginal area were 49 and in developed area were 62.

Borrower-Household Classification

It is critical for the purposes of our study to distinguish not only between production environments but also between borrowers on the basis of economic status. This type of borrower differentiation is primarily useful in drawing out the implications with respect to lenders' preferences, and in specifying the nature of credit relationships.

From the study area classification, farm households are thus further classified into three income groups. The first part of the following discussion will develop the working definition of the income groupings. The second part will examine the effect of income disparity among borrower households on repayment capacity and performance. This will then constitute the basis for our analysis of lenders' behavior, in particular their preference for certain types of borrowers. Two indicators have been used in previous empirical studies to classify borrower-households, namely: 1) land or asset ownership, and 2) income level. The first indicator is predicated on the assumption that the economic status of a farm household is determined by initial asset endowments, with land being the single most important asset of rural households. In other words, household income differences may be explained by the large disparities in control over the means of production, primarily land. Hence, one would differentiate the economic status of farm households according to the effective size of their landholdings.

Although borrowers in our theoretical model were differentiated according to landholding size, this type of classification poses problems in its application to the Survey. Differences among sample farms with respect to soil quality, topography, market accessibility, and agroclimatic considerations make standardization of effective landholdings difficult. At the same time, land markets in Philippine agriculture are undeveloped, which makes the prevailing land market prices a poor proxy for a land standardization index. This is further complicated by the different degrees of control farm households have over their land as reflected in different tenurial arrangements. For example, how does one compare the resource status of a Cagayan share tenant cultivating 4.8 hectares of rainfed land with the amortizing owner-farmer in Nueva Ecija with 1.2 hectares?

Given the difficulties in land standardization and measurement of control, we instead use the second indicator, the *household income level*, for classifying farm households in each study area into different borrower categories. There are several reasons for this. First, income inequality is a stark reality in agrarian societies, which many economists choose to ignore. And yet, as Yotopoulos and Nugent (1976) point out, the existence of poor and rich households is neither a temporary nor a transitory phenomenon.

Second, not only does income inequality exist both in the marginal as well as developed areas, it also has an important bearing on our understanding the diversity of credit terms. The income status of the farm household largely determines its bargaining position in the market, suggesting that any inter-household differences that may arise with respect to income may effect the terms and conditions of exchange in any market, including credit.

In developing a working definition of the different income groupings of the borrower-households, the following data considerations were taken into account:

1) First, a serious limitation of our household sample is the exclusion of permanent landless workers and non-cultivating landowners in the area. As a result of this omission, the income distribution profile of the sample households reflects only a microcosm of the actual distribution in the total population.

2) Second, the Survey is limited to the wet crop season, the most productive part of the year. If the Survey had covered the period between cropping seasons and the dry season, the income differences might have been wider since they would also be reflecting any differences in off-farm earning opportunities and in returns to labor during slack season.

3) And, finally, the interviews were done during 1983-84 when the province of Cagayan was experiencing severe drought. Since a large proportion of the land area remained uncultivated or yielded a poor harvest, the mean income of an average farmer was lower than usual.

The main criterion used in delineating levels of income is the relationship between minimum needs and earning capacity of the household. The following are brief descriptions of the income groupings adopted for our study purposes:

Poor households: households whose net earnings are inadequate to meet minimum subsistence needs such as food and other household expenses.

Middle households: whose net earnings are sufficient to cover subsistence needs but not special or unexpected consumption expenses, for example, education, medical expenses, and social occasions.

Rich households: whose net earnings go beyond basic needs requirements.

This classification requires the use of cut-off income levels in order to delineate households on the basis of their annualized net earnings. The first cut-off income level which differentiates poor and middle income classes is determined by the "subsistence threshold" requirement of 13,834 pesos. The second cut-off income level that differentiates middle and rich income classes, on the other hand, is equivalent to the "basic needs threshold" requirement of 23,058 pesos. In each study area, the sample households are thus further grouped into three income classes. Households with annualized total net incomes falling below 6,500 pesos for 1983-84 are classified as *poor* households. *Middle* income households comprise those with annualized income earnings between 6,501 pesos and 13,000 pesos. Those households with earnings beyond 13,001 pesos are classified in the *rich* income category.

This approach certainly has its limitations, particularly in drawing a sharp distinction between subsistence expenditures and basic needs expenditures. The principle on which the classification is based, however — namely, the household's ability to cover its needs — is important in determining the borrower's risk and repayment capacity.

Bibliography

Abbott, J.C. 1967. "The Development of Marketing Institutions," in Herman M. Southworth and Bruce F. Johnston, eds., *Agricultural Development and Economic Growth*. Pp. 364-398. Ithaca, New York: Cornell University Press.

Adams, Dale W. 1984. "Are the Arguments for Cheap Agricultural Credit Sound?" in Dale. W. Adams, D. H. Graham, and J.D. Von Pischke, eds., *Undermining Rural Development with Cheap Credit*. Pp. 65-77. Boulder, Colorado: Westview Press.

Agabin, Meliza *et al.* 1989. "Integrative Report on the Informal Credit Markets in the Philippines." Working Paper Series No. 89-10. Manila: Philippine Institute for Development Studies.

Ahmed, Z.U. 1982. "Transactions Costs in Rural Financial Markets in Bangladesh." Ph.D. Thesis, University of Virginia, Charlottesville.

Agricultural Policy and Strategy Team (APST). 1986. "Agenda for Action for the Philippine Rural Sector: A Summary." Los Baños: University of the Philippines, Agricultural Policy Research Program and the Philippine Institute of Development Studies.

Arrow, Kenneth J. 1974. *The Limits of Organization*. New York: Norton.

Asian Development Bank (ADB). 1983. *Regional Seminar on Financing of Low Income Housing: A Summary Report*. Manila: ADB.

_____ . 1985. *Improving Domestic Resources Mobilization Through Financial Development*. Manila: ADB.

Bardhan, Pranab K., ed. 1989a. *The Economic Theory of Agrarian Institutions*. Oxford: Clarendon Press.

_____ . 1989b. " Alternative Approaches to the Theory of Institutions in Economic Development," in Pranab K. Bardhan, ed., *The Economic Theory of Agrarian Institutions*. Pp. 4-17. Oxford: Clarendon Press.

_____ . 1989c. "A Note on Interlinked Rural Economic Arrangements," in Pranab K. Bardhan, ed., *The Economic Theory of Agrarian Institutions*. Pp. 237-242. Oxford:

Clarendon Press.

Basu, Kaushik. 1984a. "Implicit Interest Rates, Usury and Isolation in Backward Agriculture." *Cambridge Journal of Economics* 8 (June): 145-161.

_____. 1984b. *Less Developed Economy: A Critique of Contemporary Theory.* London: Basil Blackwell.

_____. 1987. "Disneyland Monopoly, Interlinkage and Various Interest Rates." *Journal of Public Economics* 34 (October): 1-17.

_____. 1989. "Rural Credit Markets: The Structure of Interest Rates, Exploitation, and Efficiency," in Pranab K. Bardhan, ed., *The Economic Theory of Agrarian Institutions.* Pp. 147-165. Oxford: Clarendon Press.

Baumol, William. 1976. *Economic Theory and Operations Analysis.* New Jersey: Prentice-Hall.

Bell, Clive. 1988. "Credit Markets and Interlinked Transactions," in Hollis B. Chenery and T.N. Srinivasan, eds., *Handbook of Development Economics*, Vol. 1. Pp. 763-830. Amsterdam: Elsevier Science Publishers.

Bell, Clive and T.N. Srinivasan. 1989. "Some Aspects of Linked Product and Credit Market Contracts Among Risk-neutral Agents," in Pranab Bardhan, ed., *The Economic Theory of Agrarian Institutions.* Pp. 221-236. Oxford: Clarendon Press.

Bhaduri, Amit. 1973. "Agricultural Backwardness Under Semi-feudalism." *Economic Journal* 83 (March): 120-137.

_____. 1977. "On the Formation of Usurious Interest Rates in Backward Agriculture." *Cambridge Journal of Economics* 1 (December): 341-352.

Bharadwaj, Krishna. 1985. "A View on Commercialization in Indian Agriculture and the Development of Capitalism." *Journal of Peasant Studies* 12 (July): 7-25.

Biggs, T. 1988. "Financing the Emergence of Small and Medium Enterprise in Taiwan: Heterogeneous Firm Size and Efficient Intermediation." Employment and Enterprise Development Division Discussion Paper No. 16. Washington D.C.: United States Agency for International Development.

Binswanger, Hans. 1978. "Attitudes Towards Risk: Implications for Economic and Psychological Theories of an Experiment in Rural India." Center Discussion Paper No. 286. New Haven: Economic Growth Center, Yale University.

_____. 1982. "Risk Aversion, Collateral Requirements and the Markets for Credit and Insurance in Rural Areas." Studies in Employment and Rural Development Series No. 79. Washington D.C.: The World Bank.

Blejer, Mario, I. and Jose Gil Diaz. 1986. "Interest Rate Determination in an Open Economy: the case of Uruguay." *Economic Development and Cultural Change* 34 (April): 589-606.

Bliss, Cristopher J. and Nicholas H. Stern. 1982. *Palanpur: The Economy of an Indian Village.* New Delhi: Oxford University Press.

Bottomley, Anthony. 1963. "The Premium for Risks as a Determinant of Interest Rates in Underdeveloped Rural Areas." *Quarterly Journal of Economics* 77 (November): 637-647.

_____. 1964. "Monopoly Profit as a Determinant of Interest Rates in Underdeveloped Rural Areas." *Oxford Economic Papers* 16 (October): 431-437.

Bouis, Howarth. 1982. "Rice Policy in the Philippines." Ph.D. Thesis, Stanford University, Stanford.

Braverman, Avishay and J.L. Guasch. 1984. "Capital Requirements, Screening and Interlinked Sharecropping and Credit Contracts." *Journal of Development Economics* 14 (April): 359-374.

Braverman, Avishay and T.N. Srinivasan. 1981. "Credit and Sharecropping in Agrarian Societies." *Journal of Development Economics* 9 (December): 289-312.

Braverman, Avishay and Joseph E. Stiglitz. 1982. "Sharecropping and the Interlinking of Agrarian Markets." *American Economic Review* 72 (September): 695-715.

Broad, R. 1988. *Unequal Alliance: The IMF, World Bank, and the Philippines.* Berkeley, California: University of California Press.

Bull, Clive. 1983. "Implicit Contracts in the Absence of Enforcement and Risk Aversion." *American Economic Review* 73 (September): 658-671.

Bureau of Census and Statistics, Philippines. 1962. *PSSII Bulletin Series 12.* Manila: Philippines.

Bureau of Lands, Philippines. 1980. *Manual for Land Surveys in the Philippines.* Manila: Philippines.

Burkner, H. 1980. "Savings Mobilization Through Financial Development: A Study of Savings in the Philippines." *The Philippine Economic Journal* 19 (3-4): 451-482.

Business Day. 1984. "Poverty Thresholds." *Business Day* 18 (May). Manila.

Cairncross, Alec K. 1962. *Factors in Economic Development.* London: George Allen and Unwin.

Calvo, Guillermo A. 1986. "Fractured Liberalism: Argentina under Martinez de Hoz", *Economic Development and Cultural Change*, 34 (April): 511-533.

Central Bank of the Philippines. 1974. *Twenty-Five Years of Economic and Financial Statistics in the Philippines*. Manila: Central Bank of the Philippines.

_____. 1976—. *Central Bank Annual Report*. (Various years.) Manila: Central Bank of the Philippines.

_____. 1983—. *Philippine Financial Statistics*. (Various years.) Manila: Central Bank of the Philippines.

_____. 1986. "Presidential Decree 717." Memorandum Circular. Manila: Central Bank of the Philippines.

Chaturvedi, J.M. 1959. *Theory of Marketing in Underdeveloped Countries*. Allabad: Kitab Mahal.

Cho, Yoon-Je and Deena Khatkhate. 1989. "Lessons of Financial Liberalization in Asia: A Comparative Study." World Bank Discussion Paper No. 50. Washington, D.C.: The World Bank.

Collier, Paul and Deepak Lal. 1985. *Labor and Poverty in Kenya: 1900-1980*. London: Oxford University Press.

Dalisay, A. 1937. "Types of Tenancy Contracts on Rice Farms in Nueva Ecija." *Philippine Agriculturist* 26 (2): 159-198.

Datta, Samar K. and Jeffrey B. Nugent. 1989. "Transaction Cost Economics and Contractual Choice: Theory and Evidence," in Mustapha K. Nabli and Jeffrey B. Nugent, eds., *The New Institutional Economics and Development: Theory and Applications to Tunisia*. Pp. 34-79. Amsterdam: North Holland.

David, Cristina. 1982. "Credit and Rice Policies in Philippine Agriculture." Discussion Paper Series No. 82-2. Manila: Philippine Institute for Development Studies.

Davis, William G. 1968. "Economic Limitations and Social Relationships in a Philippine Marketplace: Capital Accumulation in a Peasant Economy," in Robert van Niel, ed., *Economic Factors in Southeast Asian Social Change*. University of Hawaii Publication No. 2. Honolulu: Center for Asian and Pacific Studies, University of Hawaii.

de Alessi, Louis. 1983. "Property Rights, Transactions Costs and X-Efficiency." *American Economic Review* 73 (March): 64-81.

de Guzman, Leopoldo. 1987. "Comments on the Credit Review." Paper presented at the Workshop on Rural Financial Market Research, Central Bank of the Philippines, Manila (January 6).

Diaz-Alejandro, Carlos. 1985. "Goodbye Financial Repression, Hello Financial Crash." *Journal of Development Economics* 19 (September): 1-24.

Doherty, J.F. 1982. "Who Controls the Philippine Economy: Some Need Not Try as Hard as Others." Philippine Studies Occasional Paper No. 5. Honolulu: Center for Asian and Pacific Studies, University of Hawaii.

Eliasson, Gunnar, ed. 1986. *The Economics of Institutions and Markets.* Stockholm: Industrial Institute for Economic and Social Research.

Esguerra, Emmanuel. 1981. "The Redistributive Potential of the Masagana-99 Credit Subsidy." Master's Thesis, University of the Philippines, Diliman, Quezon City.

Floro, S.L. 1987. "Credit Relations and Market Interlinkage in Philippine Agriculture." Ph.D. Thesis, Stanford University, Stanford.

Freimer, Marshall and Myron Gordon. 1965. "Why Bankers Ration Credit." *Quarterly Journal of Economics* 79 (August): 397-416.

Fry, Maxwell J. 1978. "Money and Capital of Financial Deepening in Economic Development?" *Journal of Money, Credit and Banking* 10 (November): 464-475.

_____. 1988. *Money, Interest and Banking in Economic Development.* Baltimore: The Johns Hopkins University Press.

Gangopadhyay, Shubhashis and Kunal Sengupta. 1986. "Interlinkages in Rural Markets." *Oxford Economic Papers* 38 (March): 112-121.

_____ and _____ . 1987. "Small Farmers, Moneylenders, and Trading Activity." *Oxford Economic Papers* 39 (June): 333-342.

Gapud, J. 1958. "Financing Lowland Rice Farming in Selected Barrios of Munoz, Nueva Ecija 1957-58." Undergraduate Thesis, University of the Philippines, Los Baños.

Geron, Ma. Piedad. 1988. "Philippine Rural Credit Markets." Paper presented at the Workshop on Policy Consideration for Structural Changes and Development in the Agricultural Sector. Los Baños: University of the Philippines, Los Baños.

Ghate, P.B. 1986. "Some Issues for the Regional Study on Informal Credit Markets." Background Discussion Paper for the Design Workshop. Manila: Asian Development Bank.

Giovannini, Alberto. 1985. "Saving and the Real Interest Rate in LDCs." *Journal of Development Economics* 18 (August): 197-218.

Goldsmith, Raymond W. 1969. *Financial Structure and Development.* New Haven,

Connecticut: Yale University Press.

Gonzales-Vega, Claudio. 1984a. "Cheap Agricultural Credit: Redistribution in Reverse" in Dale. W. Adams, D. H. Graham, and J. D. Von Pischke, eds., *Undermining Rural Development with Cheap Credit*. Pp. 120-132. Boulder, Colorado: Westview Press.

_____. 1984b. "Credit Rationing Behavior of Agricultural Lenders: The Iron Law of Interest-Rate Restrictions" in Dale W. Adams, D. H. Graham, and J.D. Von Pischke, eds., *Undermining Rural Development with Cheap Credit*. Pp. 78-95. Boulder, Colorado: Westview Press.

Gurley, John and Edward Shaw. 1967. "Financial Development and Economic Development." *Economic Development and Cultural Change* 15 (April): 257-268.

Hayami, Yujiro and M. Kikuchi. 1982. *Asian Village Economy at the Crossroads*. Baltimore: John Hopkins University Press.

Hymer, Stephen and Stephen Resnick. 1969. "A Model of an Agrarian Economy with Nonagricultural Activities." *American Economic Review* 59 (September): 493-506.

IBON Databank. 1983. *The Philippine Financial System: A Primer*. Manila: IBON Databank.

Institute of Small-Scale Industries (ISSI). 1980. "A Study on the Mortality Rate and Causes of Failure of Small-Scale Industries in the Philippines." Occasional Paper. Quezon City: University of the Philippines.

_____. 1985. "Financial Factors in Small and Medium Enterprise Improvement in the Philippines." Occasional Paper. Quezon City: University of the Philippines.

International Labor Office (ILO). 1972. *Employment, Incomes and Equality: A Strategy for Increasing Productive Employment in Kenya*. Geneva: ILO.

Intrilligator, Michael D. 1971. *Mathematical Optimization and Economic Theory*. Engelwood Cliffs, New Jersey: Prentice-Hall.

Isaac, R. Mark and Vernon L. Smith. 1985. "In Search of Predatory Pricing." *Journal of Political Economy* 93 (April): 320-345.

Jaffe, Dwight and Thomas Russell. 1976. "Imperfect Information, Uncertainty, and Credit Rationing." *Quarterly Journal of Economics* 90 (November): 651-666.

Jagannathan, N. Vijay. 1987. *Informal Markets in Developing Countries*. Oxford: Oxford University Press.

James, W. 1982. "Credit Rationing, Rural Savings and Financial Policy in Developing Countries." Asian Development Bank Economic Staff Paper No. 13. Manila: Asian Development Bank.

Kaldor, Nicholas. 1963a. "Taxation for Economic Development." *Journal of Modern African Studies* 1 (March): 7-23.

_____. 1963b. "Will Underdeveloped Countries Learn to Tax?" *Foreign Affairs* 41 (January): 410-419.

Keren, Michael and David Lehvari. 1983. "The Internal Organization of the Firm and the Shape of Average Costs." *Bell Journal of Economics* 14 (Autumn): 474-486.

Keyes, W. 1982. "Approaches to Financing of Unconventional Housing: Informal Systems." Paper presented at the Regional Seminar on Financing of Low-Income Housing, Asian Development Bank, Manila (February 7-12).

Keyes, W. and M.C. Burcroft. 1976. "Housing the Urban Poor — Nonconventional Approaches to a National Problem." Institute of Philippine Culture Poverty Research Series No. 4. Quezon City: Ateneo de Manila University.

Khasnabis, R. and J. Chakravarty. 1982. "Tenancy, Credit and Agrarian Backwardness — Results of a Field Survey." Section on Review of Agriculture. *Economic and Political Weekly* 27 (March): A21-A32.

Kierkvliet, Ben. 1977. *The Huk Rebellion*. Berkeley, California: University of California Press.

Krueger, Anne. 1974. "The Political Economy of the Rent-Seeking Society." *American Economic Review* 64 (June): 291-303.

Lamberte, Mario. 1985. "Financial Liberalization and the Internal Structure of Capital Markets: The Philippine Case." Staff Paper Series No. 8507. Manila: Philippine Institute for Development Studies.

_____. 1987. "Comparative Bank Study: A Background Paper." Working Paper Series No. 87-04. Manila, Philippines: Philippine Institute for Development Studies.

_____. 1988. "The Urban Informal Credit Markets: An Integrative Report." Working Paper Series No. 88-25. Manila: Philippine Institute for Development Studies.

Lamberte, Mario and Ma. Theresa Bunda. 1988. "The Financial Markets in Low-Income Urban Communities: The Case of Sapang Palay." Working Paper Series No. 89-10. Manila: Philippine Institute for Development Studies.

Lamberte, Mario and J. Lim. 1987. "Rural Financial Markets: A Review of Literature." Staff Paper Series No. 8702. Manila: Philippine Institute for Development Studies.

Langlois, Richard N., ed. 1986. *Economics as a Process: Essays in the New Institutional Economics*. New York: Cambridge University Press.

Lewis, W. Arthur. 1954. "Economic Development with Unlimited Supplies of Labour." *Manchester School of Economic and Social Studies* 22 (May): 139-191.

Manto, J.M. and R.E. Torres. 1974. "Sources of Cost of Credit to Rice Farmers in Central Luzon." Occasional Paper. Manila: Department of Agriculture.

McKinnon, Ronald I. 1973. *Money and Capital in Economic Development*. Washington D.C.: The Brookings Institution.

McLennan, M. 1980. *The Central Luzon Plain: Land and Society in the Inland Frontier*. Quezon City: Alemar-Phoenix Publishing House.

Mitra, Pradeep K. 1983. "A Theory of Interlinked Rural Transactions." *Journal of Public Economics* 20 (March): 167-191.

Modigliani, Franco. 1986. "Life Cycle, Individual Thrift, and the Wealth of Nations." *American Economic Review* 76 (June): 297-313.

Nabli, Mustapha K. and Jeffrey B. Nugent, eds. 1989a. *The New Institutional Economics and Development: Theory and Applications to Tunisia*. Amsterdam: North Holland.

_____ and _____. 1989b. "Collective Action, Institutions and Development," in Mustapha K. Nabli and Jeffrey B. Nugent, eds., *The New Institutional Economics and Development: Theory and Applications to Tunisia*. Pp. 80-137. Amsterdam: North Holland.

Nagaraj, K. 1985. "Marketing Structures for Paddy and Arecanut in South Kanara: A Comparison of Markets in a Backward Agricultural District," in K.N. Raj *et al.*, ed., *Essays on the Commercialization of Indian Agriculture*. Oxford: University Press. Pp. 247-292.

National Economic and Development Authority (NEDA). 1984. *Philippine Statistical Yearbook*. Manila: NEDA.

Patrick, Hugh. 1966. "Financial Development and Economic Growth in Underdeveloped Countries." *Economic Development and Cultural Change* 14 (January): 174-189.

Peattie, Lisa. 1987. "An Idea in Good Currency and How It Grew: The Informal Sector." *World Development* 15 (July): 851-860.

Presidential Committee on Agricultural Credit (PCAC). 1977. "Financing Agricultural Development: The Action Program (Agricultural Credit Plan 1977-1982)."

Occasional Paper. Manila: PCAC.

Quiñones, Benjamin. 1982. "Explaining Variations in Interest Rates in Informal Rural Financial Markets in the Philippines." Master's Thesis, University of the Philippines, Los Baños.

Ray, Debraj and Kunal Sengupta. 1989. "Interlinkages and the Pattern of Competition," in Pranab Bardhan, ed., *The Economic Theory of Agrarian Institutions.* Pp. 243-263. Oxford: Clarendon Press.

Rosen, Sherwin. 1982. "Authority, Control, and the Distribution of Earnings." *Bell Journal of Economics* 13 (Autumn): 311-323.

Russell, S. 1985. "Middlemen and Moneylending: Personalized Trade and Credit in Upland Luzon, Philippines." Occasional Paper. Quezon City: School of Economics, University of the Philippines.

Sacay, Orlando. 1961. "An Analysis of the Crop Loan Program to the Agricultural Credit and Cooperative Financing Administration." Ph.D. Thesis, Cornell University, Ithaca.

Sacay, Orlando, Meliza Agabin, and C.I. Tanchoco. 1985. *Small Farmer Credit Dilemma.* Manila: Technical Board for Agricultural Credit (TBAC).

Sah, Raj Kumar and Joseph E. Stiglitz. 1986. "The Architecture of Economic Systems: Hierarchies and Polyarchies." *American Economic Review* 76 (September): 716-727.

Scherer, Frederic. 1980. *Industrial Market Structure and Economic Performance.* Chicago: Rand McNally.

Serrano, S. 1983. "The Economics of Linking Credit to Other Markets in Camarines Sur, Bicol Region, Philippines." Master's Thesis, University of the Philippines, Los Baños.

Shaw, Edward. 1973. *Financial Deepening in Economic Development.* New York: Oxford University Press.

Silverio, S. 1982. "The Neighborhood Sari-Sari Store." *The Philippine Poor I: Two Monographs.* Quezon City: Institute of Philippine Culture, Ateneo de Manila University.

Social Security Service (SSS), Philippines. 1980. *Annual Report: Year Ended December 31, 1980.* Quezon City: Social Security System.

Stiglitz, Joseph E. and Andrew Weiss. 1981. "Credit Rationing in Markets with Imperfect Information." *American Economic Review* 71 (June): 393-410.

_____ and _____. 1983. "Incentive Effects of Terminations: Applications to the Credit and Labor Markets." *American Economic Review* 73 (December): 912-927.

Swaminathan, Madhura. 1982. "The Study of the Credit Behavior of Farm Families in Nueva Ecija." Agricultural Economics Department Paper No. 82-27. Los Baños: International Rice Research Institute.

Szanton, Maria Cristina. 1972. *A Right to Survive—Subsistence Marketing in a Lowland Philippine Town.* University Park and London: Pennsylvania State University Press.

Tan, Edita. 1980. "Philippine Monetary Policy and Aspects of the Financial Market: A Review of the Literature." Survey of Philippine Development Research. Manila: Philippine Institute for Development Studies.

Technical Board for Agricultural Credit (TBAC). 1981. *A Study of the Informal Rural Financial Markets in Three Selected Provinces in the Philippines.* Manila: Presidential Committee on Agricultural Credit.

_____. 1985. *Agricultural Credit Study.* Manila: Presidential Committee on Agricultural Credit.

_____. 1986. "Small Farm Indebtedness Survey." *National Report* 1 (June).

Technical Board for Agricultural Credit and UP Business Research Foundation (TBAC-UPBRF). 19 . "Financing Integrated Development in the Rural Community: Focus on the Masagana-99." Revised Report. Quezon City: University of the Philippines, Business Research Foundation, Inc.

Thorbecke, Erik. 1988. "Institutions, X-Efficiency, Transactions Costs and Socioeconomic Development." Paper presented at the Conference on Efficiency, Internal Organization and Comparative Management. Bellagio, Italy.

Timberg, Thomas and C.V. Aiyar. 1984. "Informal Credit Markets in India." *Economic Development and Cultural Change* 33 (October): 43-59.

Todaro, Michael. 1968. "A Model of Labor Migration and Urban Unemployment in Less Developed Countries." *American Economic Review* 59 (March): 138-148.

Tolentino, Bruce. 1986. "Current Imperatives and Developments in Philippine Agricultural Credit Policy." Occasional Paper. Manila: Agricultural Credit Policy Council.

Torres, A. 1984. "Survival Entrepreneurship Carries Day for Thousands of Metro Manilans." *Depthnews* 6 (November): Pp. 1-6.

Umbeck, John. 1981. *A Theory of Property Rights.* Ames, Iowa: Iowa State University Press.

Umbeck, John and Robert Chatfield. 1982. "The Structure of Contracts and Transactions Costs." *Journal of Money, Credit and Banking* 14 (November): 511-516.

Van Atta, Sue. 1971. "A Note on Usury Legislation in the Philippines." *The Philippine Economic Journal* 10 (1): 48-62.

Von Pischke, J.D. and Dale Adams. 1983. "Fungibility and the Design and Evaluation of Agricultural Credit Markets," in J. D. Von Pischke *et al.*, eds., *Rural Financial Markets in Developing Countries*. Pp. 74-83. Baltimore: John Hopkins University Press.

Von Weizsacker, Carl. 1980. *Barriers to Entry: A Theoretical Treatment*. Berlin and New York: Springer-Verlag.

Wai, U Tun. 1956. "Interest Rates in the Organized Money Markets of Underdeveloped Countries." *International Monetary Fund Staff Papers* 5 (August): 249-268.

_____. 1957. "Interest Rates Outside the Organized Money Markets of Underdeveloped Countries." *International Monetary Fund Staff Papers*, 6 (November): 80-142.

_____. 1977. "A Revisit to Interest Rates Outside the Organized Money Markets of Underdeveloped Countries." *Banca Nazionale del Lavoro Quarterly Review* 122 (September): 291-312.

Williamson, Oliver E. 1975. *Markets and Hierarchies: Analysis and Antitrust Implications*. New York: Free Press.

_____. 1987. "Kenneth Arrow and the New Institutional Economics," in George Feiwel, ed., *Arrow and the Foundations of the Theory of Economic Policy*. Pp. 584-599. New York: New York University Press.

Yotopoulos, Pan A. and Jeffrey B. Nugent. 1976. *Economics of Development: Empirical Investigations*. New York: Harper and Row.

Yotopoulos, Pan A. 1988. "The (Rip)Tide of Privatization: Lessons from Chile." *World Development* 17 (May): 683-702.

_____. 1989. "Trade and Foreign-Owned Production in Services: Some Conceptual and Theoretical Issues," in H. Giersch, ed., *Services in World Economic Growth*. Pp. 151-155. Tubingen, Germany: J.C.B. Mohr (Paul Siebeck).

Index